OUT OF OUR
IRRITATIONS HE
BRINGS FORTH
PEARLS

Give GOD the Ashes

CHRISTINE MENSCH

Belleville, Ontario, Canada

GIVE GOD THE ASHES
Copyright © 2009, Christine Mensch

All Rights Reserved. No part of this publication may be reproduced, stored in a retrieval system or transmitted in any form or by any means—electronic, mechanical, photocopy, recording or any other— except for brief quotations in printed reviews, without the prior permission of the author.

All scripture quotations unless otherwise marked are taken from the New King James Version. Copyright © 1979, 1980, 1982. Thomas Nelson Inc., Publishers.

ISBN: 978-1-55452-405-1
LSI Edition: 978-1-55452-406-8

**For more information or
to order additional copies, please contact:**

Christine Mensch
29-284 Cougar Way North
Lethbridge, AB T1H 6T9

Essence Publishing is a Christian Book Publisher dedicated to furthering the work of Christ through the written word.
For more information, contact:
20 Hanna Court, Belleville, Ontario, Canada K8P 5J2.
Phone: 1-800-238-6376. Fax: (613) 962-3055.
E-mail: info@essence-publishing.com
Web site: www.essence-publishing.com

Printed in Canada
by

Essence
PUBLISHING

Contents

Dedication and Acknowledgements 7
Preface 9

SECTION 1

Diligence 13
Patience 17
Overcoming Evil by Doing Good 23
Forgetting Our Negative Past and Moving on to Fruitfulness 29
Purity 33
Wisdom 37
Authority 41
The Lord, the Shepherd, Restores Our Souls 47
Loneliness 51
Fear 55
Uncertainty 61
Dread 65
Physical Pain 69
Weariness 75
The Dark Times 79
Preparation 85

Freedom	91
Grief	97
Joy	101
Peace	105
Health	109
Guilt	115
How to Be Used by God Without Being Used by People	121
A True Servant of the Living God	125
Strength	129
Hope	135
Silence	139
Pearls	141
Meditation and Studying	143
Knowledge	145
Principles	149
Reputation	151
Faithfulness	155
Self-Control	159
Excellent Spirit	161
Time	165
Disappointment	169
Depression	171
Frustration	173
Drudgery	175
Procrastination	177
Rejection	179
Encouragement	183

Presumptuousness 185
Strongholds 187
Healthy Relationships 191
Friendship 195
Repentance 199
Perseverance 203
The Blood of Jesus 205

SECTION 2
My Journey through the Valleys 209
The Snow-Covered Mountain 231
The Indefinable Valley 233
The Promise of God 235
Interlude with God 237
The Canoes in the River 239
The Concrete Wall 241
The Clear Water 243
The Hammer of God 245
Inevitable Changes 247
The Christmas Season 251
The New Year 253
Lush Green Foliage 255
Eagles Wings 257
Conclusion 259
Epilogue 269

Dedication and Acknowledgments

To my wonderful sisters, Eva, Anne, Mary, and Helen, I express my gratitude for your constant support, encouragement, and prayers. You are the best! It means more to me than you will ever know. Once again, I say thanks for your constant prayers, which helped to produce in writing the pearls gleaned from the ashes of my life.

My first love, praise, and dedication of this book go to my Lord and Savior, Jesus Christ. It is my prayer and desire that through the inspiration He gave me for these writings He will make them a blessing to touch the hearts of those who read them.

I dedicate this book also to my precious grandson, Jackson David DeLong, born March 13, 2008. Jackson, may God's hand be upon your life always, and may you know Him intimately and walk in His ways all the days of your life. You are truly a blessing from God, and your arrival brought great joy into our lives. We love you more than words can say! I pray that you will be a man after God's own heart whose character reflects that of Jesus.

I dedicate these writings also to Jackson's beautiful older sister, Olivia Katherine, born August 12, 2006. You are also a great blessing and a joy to all of us. We love you from the depths of our hearts! You were born while I wrote my first book, and your brother came while I was writing this one. My prayer is that you will glean some pearls from this book also. I pray that you will be a woman whose rare beauty comes from the virtues of Christ Jesus living within you.

In addition, I dedicate these writings to all who want to cultivate the fruit of the Holy Spirit and grow deeper in their walk with God. My prayer is that God will make you like an oak tree planted by the rivers of water, to bring forth its fruit in its season (Psalm 1:3).

Preface

Here I begin the writing of my second book. For years and years, I felt as though time were running out and none of the things God seemed to have put in my heart were happening. Love for God and love for the truth were burning like a fire in my heart. It was a deep longing to give expression to what God had put in my heart. It was an ache inside of me all the time.

I knew the hand of God was heavily upon me and that He had called me to something very specific, but I waited and I waited and I waited, and it was not happening. Every time I had another birthday, I felt more and more as though time were running out and the will of God was not happening in my life the way it seemed He had said. It was anguish in my soul, and I felt consumed by what He had put in my heart.

However, it seemed nothing in my life was lining up in any way with what the fire of God in my soul indicated. I wanted desperately to know and do the will of God. It should have been easy to determine, or so I thought. Then why was it so difficult?

It seemed one of the things He was asking me to do was write. If that was what He wanted me to do, then He needed to give me something in my life worth writing about. My life of drudgery would not be much of an attraction for readers. I could not imagine even putting it into words, let alone someone else wanting to read about it.

The exact opposite seemed to be happening. Detours on the road of life kept taking me in the opposite direction to what the fire of God in my heart indicated. My dreams, aspirations, and longings died repeatedly. Had I really heard God? Did He truly give me those dreams? Was this all there was to the Christian life? Was it my own desire in my heart or my imagination? Was I following an elusive rainbow? Or did God really put those things in my heart?

The years continued to go by, decades went by, and in the meantime everything turned into ashes while the fire of God slowly but surely burned the dross out of my life. It seemed all the things I longed for and hoped for came to nothing. Everything turned to ashes. Ashes are useless—unless we give those ashes to God so He can bring something out of nothing that will glorify His Name.

The inspiration for the these writings comes from the pearls He brought forth out of the things that were great irritations to me in my life. He brings forth what He desires out of the ashes. He brings freshness and newness of life out of the gloomy gray ashes of our death to self.

Galatians 2:20 says, "*I have been crucified with Christ; it is no longer I who live, but Christ lives in me; and the life which I now live in the flesh I live by faith in the Son of God, who loved me and gave Himself for me.*"

Section I

Diligence

Be diligent to present yourself approved to God, a worker who does not need to be ashamed, rightly dividing the word of truth (2 Timothy 2:15).

In the beginning was the Word, and the Word was with God, and the Word was God. He was in the beginning with God. All things were made through Him, and without Him nothing was made that was made. In Him was life, and the life was the light of men…And the Word became flesh and dwelt among us, and we beheld His glory, the glory as of the only begotten of the Father, full of grace and truth (John 1:1–4;14).

We need to go to God without preconceived ideas about what He wants us to understand. As we go to His Word we need to approach it not as another textbook but as a roadmap for life that the Author, who is God the Father, by His Spirit has revealed to us so that we can know Him and find out His ways through reading, studying and meditating on it.

In order to understand His Word, we need to know Him. The Holy Spirit opens our understanding to His Word. God the Holy Spirit is the Teacher. We need to have our understanding opened to the Word of God so that it transforms us into the very likeness of God's own Son and gives us the same heart attitudes as Jesus revealed when He was on earth. Jesus was the Word and became flesh as a human being. He was God in the flesh.

While I waited on God about what He wanted this book to say to you, the reader, He spoke to me and said, "Once again, it is time to set aside all other Christian books and read only the Bible while you are writing this book." That was God's direction for me until this book was completed. When these times come, the Bible becomes even richer to me, and I realize how life-giving God's Word is. Though God's Word is life, when we invite the Holy Spirit into our times of reading it He quickens it to our hearts so that we understand it.

I also have often had to go through times of intense loneliness when God is preparing me for another task. I long for clarity, answers and direction as well as some assurance that I am doing exactly what He is asking of me. I seek Him, and then often He seems to be silent. I long for someone to speak into my life, and it seems there is no one to turn to. No one seems to understand. I have to wait until God speaks to me and until He points the way to my next task.

In the end there is often great blessing, but in the meantime it is often agonizing when there is such a longing inside me to clearly hear and fully understand what God is doing in preparing me for what lies ahead. Often the silence lasts for extended periods. When He says nothing, I can do nothing. That does not come natural to the flesh. My flesh groans during these times.

Sometimes we are hard on ourselves during times of God's silence. We ask ourselves, Why can I not hear God's voice, and why is it so difficult for me to hear Him? What is wrong with me? The truth is that we cannot hear something He has not chosen to tell us yet. When He is not speaking, there is nothing to hear. The silence keeps us pressing in to God, and in that process He is bringing us to the end of ourselves—death to the flesh. The purpose is for the fruit of the Spirit to grow so that there will be more of Him and less of you and me. The silence bonds us to Him, and our ears become more and more ready to hear Him when He does speak. It is one way He develops our listening skills.

These things are simple, but they do not come easily. The journey is lifelong, and the more we surrender to it, the more we will become like Jesus in the process.

I sense the Spirit of God saying, "My children, come to Me and release your cares, your fears, your worries, and stop your fretting about the things you cannot change. I have come to give you peace, and I want to dwell in your hearts in peace and rest. Sit with Me, and enter into the stillness that I bring. The calm and the rest are for all who are weary and tired and long for a peace that you can only find in Me."

Patience

Therefore, having been justified by faith, we have peace with God through our Lord Jesus Christ, through whom also we have access by faith into this grace in which we stand, and rejoice in hope of the glory of God. And not only that, but we also glory in tribulations, knowing that tribulation produces perseverance; and perseverance, character; and character, hope. Now hope does not disappoint, because the love of God has been poured out in our hearts by the Holy Spirit who was given to us (Romans 5:1–5).

My brethren, count it all joy when you fall into various trials, knowing that the testing of your faith produces patience. But let patience have its perfect work, that you may be perfect and complete, lacking nothing. If any of you lacks wisdom, let him ask of God, who gives to all liberally and without reproach, and it will be given to him (James 1:2–5).

Whenever we see the word *therefore* we have to look at the previous Scripture to find out what was referred to before the word *therefore*. The previous verses (Romans 4) explain to us that Jesus made righteousness available to us through His death and resurrection. We by grace, through faith, receive what He has purchased for us by His sacrifice of giving up His life to death on the cross. His glorious resurrection three days later completed the victory.

Romans 8:11 says, "*But if the Spirit of Him who raised Jesus from the dead dwells in you, He who raised Christ from the dead will also give life to your mortal bodies through His Spirit who dwells in you.*" We now know that the same Spirit who raised Christ from the dead dwells in us, and we can overcome through His power working in us. He causes us to triumph over the troubles we face in this life. He is the hope within us that keeps us persevering until we see the answer and until our deliverance comes from whatever we are going through at the time.

Often, my prayer and my longing is "Lord, will You please take me out of this misery." Usually, He takes me *through* instead of *out of* the situation. Sometimes we need to remove ourselves from a situation that is not working any good in us. Many times God walks us through the tunnel instead of snatching us out of it. When we are in a tunnel or wilderness, we cannot see very far ahead, and that does not usually feel right or comfortable to our natural desires. God is working in us to produce the same character in us as Jesus has. That means we patiently have to wait for God to work things out in our lives, while our responsibility is to yield to the Spirit of God and obey the Word of God during the process.

There would be no purpose in making us wait just for the sake of enduring hardship. However, fruit shows or grows in us when we behave in a way that pleases God during those times. It is not just about enduring; it is all about behaving in a Christlike manner when it is not easy and when it does not come naturally to us. It is about growing in Christlikeness and producing Holy-Spirit fruit. As we choose to do what is right according to God's Word, we will triumph in our circumstances and come through victoriously.

During these times, we are becoming more like Jesus than we were before. That is the very purpose for which God allows us to experience hardships instead of just shielding us from everything that makes us uncomfortable or irritates us and frustrates us.

During the time I was writing my first book, God tested me severely in the areas I wrote about in that book. The waiting tests seemed more than I could bear, but not according to God's standards, because when He saw fit to move me on, He did it. Sometimes it was very hard for me to wait for Him when He was silent when I was so desperate to hear from Him. Yet the silence seemed to go on and on and on—as though He did not even notice what I was experiencing.

I always find very difficult when I need to explain what is going on in my life or someone asks me questions about it and the only answer I have is "I do not know." Since the Lord has not shown me what to do next or even why I am going through what I am right then, I cannot explain it to others. All I know during those times is that I cannot change it until He directs me and makes a way. These things do not seem to matter to God at the time. We need to find our confidence and our trust and hope in Him. That is the benefit of the growing experience.

One Sunday morning when I was having my devotions before I left for church I felt desperate to hear from God about many things. It seemed He had not answered me about any of those things. I had to have some things cleared up, and only He could do that. During that time, I sat quietly and listened for His voice, and then I said, "Lord, You know there are many things weighing heavily on my heart, but Heavenly Father, will You tell me what is on Your heart?" Then I sat quietly and waited for a while, and I heard Him ask me one question, with a voice that felt like "rolling thunder" in my spirit. It had nothing to do with any of the things weighing heavily on my heart. It was unexpected and had nothing to do with anything I had been talking to Him about. The words disturbed me at the time and echo in my spirit to this day. He said this to me, "Christine, will you be My disciple?"

It shook me up. I could not understand why He would ask me that. What did He mean? I thought I settled that many, many years ago. I had surrendered my life to Him without any reservations. I never had any desire to turn back. Through thick and thin I always chose to find refuge in Him and trust Him to take me through every trial. If He could not take me out of the furnace or wilderness I was in, I persevered through it with His help. Repeatedly, I asked God, "Why would You ask me that, Lord? I thought I answered this question when I chose to receive Jesus as Savior." I wondered what He meant and why He asked me such a strange question.

Often it seems God is not a Father of many words. He remained silent, and I pursued Him as I sought diligently for His explanation for the question He asked me. I listened attentively for anything He might say.

As time went on, I did not forget it but continually listened for His answer to come so that I would know why He asked me something so disturbing to me. It took several months, but one day I began to understand. He was asking me if I would do what He asks me to and follow what He is saying even if I do not see anyone else around me doing that and even if other teachers are not telling me the things He is.

One of the things He brought back to my mind was a dream I had years ago. In the dream I was in a waiting room, and it was a place of learning. There were bookshelves on the walls, and I had notepaper in front of me. It had nothing written on it at the time. The only thing in front of me was my Bible and the notepaper. I wrote in more detail about this dream in my first book, *Keep It Simple, Saints,* which is subtitled *How to Develop a Listening Ear for God's Voice.* Though the message in the dream affected me deeply at the time, I did not have any idea what it truly meant. Now I clearly understand that I was in the preparation school of the Holy

Spirit Himself. After all these years, my time to write has finally come, and my inspiration must come from God Himself. When He asked me if I am willing to be His disciple He wanted me to understand that I am to rely totally on Him to tell me what to write instead of using many study resources. My answer needed to be "Yes, Lord; You are my Master and my Teacher." He was asking me to surrender even more fully to His training and allow Him to teach me by His Spirit. He allowed me only the Bible and the Holy Spirit as my sources. He was asking me if I was willing to be His student in the school of the Holy Spirit.

I believe the Holy Spirit wants to encourage all of you who have been patiently waiting for the things God put in your hearts long ago. You wonder if you heard wrong or why things just do not seem to fall into place the way you believed they would. Do not lose heart, for you will see the promise of God and the vision happen if you continue to yield to the work of the Holy Spirit within you.

Sometimes we have to die to our dreams before we see them come to fruition, and sometimes we have to die to them more than once. Some of you have very definite calls and some very great tasks God is preparing you for, so do not be discouraged. Press in to God Himself, and when you least expect it, it will happen. Let patience have its perfect way in you. The greater the call, the greater the refining process in our lives has to be. It is necessary. God Himself prepares the vessel for His use before He can pour out His love through that vessel the way He longs to do.

When God gives a vision for the things He is training and equipping us for, our minds immediately go to work, and we form a mental picture of how this is going to look. However, if what we have is truly from God, when He brings it to pass it will look very different from the mental picture we formed of it at first. Once the Spirit of God has completed the work in us and then performs what He has worked in us, it is clearly the work of the Holy Spirit, and first the flesh or the old carnal nature has to die. Yet when God first begins to speak to us about it, the flesh is very eager to see it happen, and often we become very impatient. However, timing is always very important, and we must be attentive to the Holy Spirit and always be obedient to what He says. It is very important to wait for Him.

We can learn from the example of others, such as Sarah and Abraham. They decided to help God bring to pass what He had promised them when He said they would have an heir (Genesis 16). They worked it out themselves, and it had some lifelong consequences for them. We must wait for God to bring it to pass and not try to make it happen in our own strength.

Overcoming Evil by Doing Good

Let love be without hypocrisy. Abhor what is evil. Cling to what is good. Be kindly affectionate to one another with brotherly love, in honor giving preference to one another; not lagging in diligence, fervent in spirit, serving the Lord; rejoicing in hope, patient in tribulation, continuing steadfastly in prayer; distributing to the needs of the saints, given to hospitality. Bless those who persecute you; bless and do not curse. Rejoice with those who rejoice, and weep with those who weep. Be of the same mind toward one another. Do not set your mind on high things, but associate with the humble. Do not be wise in your own opinion. Repay no one evil for evil. Have regard for good things in the sight of all men. If it is possible, as much as depends on you, live peaceably with all men. Beloved, do not avenge yourselves, but rather give place to wrath; for it is written, "Vengeance is Mine, I will repay," says the Lord. Therefore "If your enemy is hungry, feed him; If he is thirsty, give him a drink; For in so doing you will heap coals of fire on his head." Do not be overcome by evil, but overcome evil with good (Romans 12:9–21).

In Matthew 5:43–48 Jesus said,

"You have heard that it was said, 'You shall love your neighbor and hate your enemy.' But I say to you, love your

enemies, bless those who curse you, do good to those who hate you, and pray for those who spitefully use you and persecute you, that you may be sons of your Father in heaven; for He makes His sun rise on the evil and on the good, and sends rain on the just and on the unjust. For if you love those who love you, what reward have you? Do not even the tax collectors do the same? And if you greet your brethren only, what do you do more than others? Do not even the tax collectors do so? Therefore you shall be perfect, just as your Father in heaven is perfect."

Where does this kind of motivation come from? Is it possible to live this way? Does God actually require us to do good deeds to or speak well of someone who has wronged us or maybe spoken evil about us? This Scripture clearly tells us so. Whatever the Lord tells us is always for our own good. This is the way we overcome the obstacles and traps that Satan sets for us on the pathway we walk in this life.

As we choose to do this, we learn the secrets of God. It is not natural, of course, and in the eyes of many people it is not normal. They may even think there is something wrong with us if we repay an unkind act with an act of kindness. God says if we do this we make room for Him to take revenge.

We entangle ourselves in more than a verbal or physical battle if we try to get even or take revenge ourselves. We engage or entangle ourselves in a spiritual battle, which we cannot win on our own. The devil fuels these kinds of battles, and he loves to set us up for them. We need God to intervene, and we need to get out of His way. We have to get out of the way, and then He will bring about good out of the situation for us. If we leave room for God to work in the situation, we are conquerors and God will reward us.

God always rewards those who overcome evil by repaying an

evil act with a righteous one. It does not mean that we will not feel like taking revenge and getting even, so to speak. It does not mean that we will not have emotions that tell us otherwise. We act according to what God's Word says, not according to how we feel about it.

We learn these "kingdom secrets" by practicing what the Word of God says. For example, someone tells you that someone else has said something about you that is false and very unkind, and it hurts deeply. Something inside you will rise up and want revenge, but if you set out to fight the battle with your own words or earthly weapons instead of asking God to take over, you will become embroiled in something ugly. It is like adding fuel to a fire that is burning. Do not do it! Spare yourself the grief and ask God to show you how to do what the Word of God says to do in these situations. You wonder how I know this—because I have done both!

When we try to get even or fight back, the situation often intensifies or gets far worse. This is a time to seek the Lord, ask for strength to overcome with His help, and ask Him to guide us into obeying His Word. That is not an easy thing to do, but once we learn the rewards and the peace that comes with having done that, it becomes a lot easier. Proverbs 25:22 tells us that if we do what these Scriptures tell us we will be heaping coals of fire on our enemy's head and the Lord will reward us for it.

When we really feel the need for revenge against someone else, the part about heaping coals of fire on his or her head might sound "delicious" to us, but it is referring to an act of kindness to that individual. It is not literally about scorching his or her head with hot coals.

When we refuse to take revenge ourselves, we spare ourselves a lot of trouble. We move into God's protection if we leave it up to Him. His Word clearly says that if we do not try to take revenge and we choose to return good for evil, then God will take revenge.

We will be overcome by the evil if we take matters into our own hands, but if we refuse to retaliate, then God will reward us, and He will take revenge in His way and in His time.

The Word of God is showing us how to behave wisely, live at peace, and let God take care of the wrongs done to us. We will be consumed by the battle, rather than be free of it, if we engage in strife by trying to take revenge ourselves. God wants us to learn to do it the way His Word tells us to do it so that we can live at peace with even our enemies. Proverbs 16:7 says, *"When a man's ways please the LORD, He makes even his enemies to be at peace with him."*

As we learn to live more and more by the Word of God, we are learning what it means to dwell in the secret place of the Most High. When we live by God's Word, we are abiding in His Presence, and that is a secret place because it is not visible to the natural eye.

I hear God saying that there are many of you who have yearned for His Presence. He is here to meet with you right now. He longs to satisfy your craving for Him and to lead you into greater and greater experiences of His presence. The Word of God is the anchor, but there is nothing wrong with wanting to experience God's manifest presence and His power in our lives.

Many of you have been in a wilderness, and yet you have remained steadfast and walked with God even when it seemed dry and you felt very weary. However, this is a new day dawning for many of you, and as you draw close to Him and invite His presence, you are going to see the things you have patiently waited for all these years. Answers are coming and blessings are flowing out to you as you seek His face while you read this book.

This is merely a refreshing beginning. God has much more for you. Many of you have great callings, and there are God-ordained assignments that await you. They will come to fruition as you let go of your striving, let go of the wrongs done to you, wait in His presence, and let Him speak to you personally. Cease from the busyness of life. Find a time and meeting place with God where you meet with Him regularly, and you will enter into a new depth of understanding and purpose in your Christian life.

Some of you have been Christians for many years and have never really found the satisfaction in the Christian walk that you longed for. Now as you begin to listen for His voice, you are going to see what you have longed for, and your cups will overflow with the richness of His presence in your lives. Therefore, be diligent and patient and remember that the way to overcome evil is by doing good. Perseverance will produce good fruit in your life.

Forgetting Our Negative Past and Moving on to Fruitfulness

Joseph was thirty years old when he stood before Pharaoh king of Egypt. And Joseph went out from the presence of Pharaoh, and went throughout all the land of Egypt. Now in the seven plentiful years the ground brought forth abundantly. So he gathered up all the food of the seven years which were in the land of Egypt, and laid up the food in the cities; he laid up in every city the food of the fields which surrounded them. Joseph gathered very much grain, as the sand of the sea, until he stopped counting, for it was immeasurable. And to Joseph were born two sons before the years of famine came, whom Asenath, the daughter of Poti-Pherah priest of On, bore to him. Joseph called the name of the firstborn Manasseh: "For God has made me forget all my toil and all my father's house." And the name of the second he called Ephraim: "For God has caused me to be fruitful in the land of my affliction" (Genesis 41:46–52).

Joseph had a lot to overcome, but through it all he determined to live according to the Word of God and refused to compromise in any way, even when it meant going to prison. His brothers sold him to some Ishmaelites, who took him to Egypt, where they sold him to Potiphar, one of Pharaoh's officers. Joseph became a slave in Potiphar's house. Joseph's brothers took the coat that belonged to him and killed one of the kid goats, dipped the coat in its blood, took it to their father and asked if he recognized the coat. They deceived him into believing that a wild animal had killed Joseph (Genesis 37).

Then Potiphar's wife lied about Joseph and said that he tried to rape her. The truth was that she pursued him and he ran from her. Joseph refused to sleep with her and defile her and himself and sin against God, but he was sent to prison because of her false accusations (Genesis 39).

While he was there, he remained faithful to his God and found favor there as well. He rightly interpreted the butler's and baker's dreams and asked the butler to remember him when he was restored to his position. The butler was restored to his position, just as the interpretation to the dream indicated he would be, but promptly forgot about Joseph (Genesis 40).

For another two years Joseph remained in prison, until Pharaoh had dreams that he wanted someone to interpret and none of the magicians he called was able to do it. Then the butler remembered Joseph and how he accurately interpreted the dream he had in the prison two years earlier.

Joseph was brought before Pharaoh, and God gave him the interpretation to the dreams Pharaoh had. He also gave direction about what Pharaoh should do so there would be provision for the people during the seven years of famine that the dreams indicated were coming. When such wisdom came through Joseph, the pharaoh put Joseph in charge of making all the arrangements, making him second-in-command to the pharaoh over all the land of Egypt. Joseph went from the prison to the palace overnight (Genesis 41).

Pharaoh gave Joseph a wife, and she bore him two sons, whom they named Manasseh and Ephraim. He remained faithful to God, and now the blessings were finally coming into his life, and he named his two sons accordingly. Genesis 41:51–52 says, *"Joseph called the name of the firstborn Manasseh: 'For God has made me forget all my toil and all my father's house.' And the name of the second he called Ephraim: 'For God has caused me to be fruitful in the land of my affliction.'"*

Joseph chose to forget his negative past, all the *toil*, as he called it. The toil refers to all the trouble in his life. He moved on to the life of fruitfulness God had prepared him for. Likewise, we need to let go of negative things in our past so that we can move on to the fruitful life God wants us to live.

If Joseph could forgive and have that outlook with all the things that happened to him, then with God's help you and I can do that too.

To forget all our troubles or whatever negative experiences we have had in life does not mean we no longer have a recollection of what happened. It just means that we do not have any bitterness about them and we do not let them rob us of the future God has planned for us. If we stay close to God and keep our hearts right when tough times come, then God can bring good out of everything that happens to us. Whether it was intended for evil or not, God can use it for good if we ask Him to do that and we keep our hearts right in it.

When Jacob died, Joseph's brothers who had betrayed him all those years before and lied to their father were afraid that perhaps now Joseph would want revenge. Joseph gave them his answer as recorded in Genesis 50:19–21:

> *Joseph said to them, "Do not be afraid, for am I in the place of God? But as for you, you meant evil against me; but God meant it for good, in order to bring it about as it is this day, to save many people alive. Now therefore, do not be afraid; I will provide for you and your little ones." And he comforted them and spoke kindly to them.*

Joseph was truly a man who knew God intimately. He understood the secrets of God, and he knew where to find help for himself during the times of trouble in his life. He knew that vengeance belongs to God and it is best to leave it in God's hands. Then He will use for good what others may have intended for evil against us.

I perceive that the Lord is saying that some of you reading this think these principles may have worked for Joseph but you do not see how that could ever happen for you. Many negative things have come your way. It seems life has been cruel to you. You believe it is far too late to turn your life around now so that you could truly live a fruitful and victorious life.

Do not lose heart. God wants you to draw close to Him and ask Him to bring good out of the evil things that have been done to you. Whether it was someone else or your own mistakes or wrong reactions that brought hardships into your life, God wants you to ask Him to take charge of your life, and then you will see what He will do. God does not abandon you, and you are not without hope. However, you must surrender fully to Him, and then you will see His hand upon your life. Let go of the reins of your own life, and stop trying to do it yourself. Admit to God that you need Him desperately, and ask Him to forgive you for trying to do it on your own. Invite His Holy Spirit to order your steps, and begin to walk and talk with Him, and you will see big changes coming into your life.

Purity

"Blessed are the pure in heart, For they shall see God" (Matthew 5:8).

How can a young cleanse his way? By taking heed according to Your word. With my whole heart I have sought You; Oh, let me not wander from Your commandments! Your word I have hidden in my heart, That I might not sin against You (Psalm 119:9–11).

The words of the LORD are pure words, Like silver tried in a furnace of earth, Purified seven times (Psalm 12:6).

With the pure You will show Yourself pure; And with the devious You will show Yourself shrewd (Psalm 18:26).

Purity means cleanness.[1] It is freedom from any defilement, foreign matter, or adulterating matter—the absence of admixture. Jesus said those who are pure in heart will see God. That does not just mean we will see God in heaven one day. If our hearts are pure, we will see what God is doing all around us. We will see what He is doing in our own lives and in the lives of others. We will see things in the world around us through the eyes of the Spirit of God living within us.

---

[1] *Funk and Wagnall's Standard College Dictionary* (Fitzhenry & Whiteside Ltd., 1978).

Purity is very important. Jesus said that we speak from the abundance of our hearts (Matthew 12:34). What comes out of our mouths reveals what is in our hearts. The kinds of things we have an appetite for are a good indication of the kind of hearts we have. The kinds of things that take up our conversation reveal what is in our hearts. The things that attract us or tempt us give a true reflection of what is in our hearts.

Our motives need to be pure so that we do things for the right reasons. Do we befriend certain people because of what it will do for us? Is it because they hold a position that will make us look good? Or do we befriend people simply because we love them and care about them? Is our speech pure? Do we speak truth in love, or do we flatter people because that will give us favor in places that will benefit us?

These things are very important to God, and if we truly love God they will be very important to us as well. Jesus said that if we love Him we will keep His commandments (John 14:21). We can check our own hearts or motives by evaluating honestly how seriously we take the commandments of Jesus, and that is an exact measurement of how much we love Him. If we love Him, we will do what He says. If we take His commandments very lightly, we obviously do not love Him very much.

The aforementioned Scripture from Psalm 119 says that we keep our way pure by hiding God's Word in our hearts. The emphasis is again on the Word of God to us, which we find in the Bible of course. The Psalmist said he had hidden the Word of God in his heart so that he would not sin against Him. We hide God's Word in our hearts by reading it, meditating on it, studying and memorizing it, and applying it to our lives every day.

If we give God first place in our lives, we will have the same attitudes toward sin that He has. Though we fall short of what Jesus showed us in Himself, we do not just shrug and say, "Oh well, we all sin all the time." We have a sincere desire in our hearts not to sin against God or anyone else. The shedding of Jesus' blood was a sacrifice we should not take lightly.

If we truly love God, we desire to live a life of purity and holiness, and it grieves our own hearts when we sin. Anything that grieves the Holy Spirit grieves us, because we know that Jesus died to save us and to free us from sin's power in our lives. Therefore, we must not continue to sin willfully. He gave us His Spirit to help us overcome sin and to change our focus from obeying laws to obeying the commandments of love so that we can live as Jesus lived. We continually turn away from the old sinful nature to have God's nature increase in us. Meanwhile, the old sin or carnal nature is dying daily so that we can be more and more a reflection of Jesus on this earth.

We need to renew our minds with God's Word. This purifies our thought-life as well. We make the Word the most important reading material in our lives. This way we start to think in harmony with the Word of God, which means we are receiving the "mind of Christ," or starting to think the same way God thinks. The things we think about will influence the way we behave and who we become. When we only do things outwardly to find acceptance with people, we are conforming to a standard of behavior, but when we are renewing our minds with the Word of God we are being transformed by it into the likeness of Jesus (Romans 12:2; 2 Corinthians 3:18).

The word I am receiving from the Lord is a call to purity in all areas of our lives. He wants to sanctify us wholly, set us apart so we will be more and more a reflection of Him in these last days. He wants to shine brightly through His Church, the people of God, but there has been much defilement in the body of Christ, and it is grieving God's Holy Spirit. The sin grieves Him because it keeps the Church from His power. He wants the Church to reveal by their actions what God is like. He wants the Church to shine as a very bright light in a dark place. When the Church blends in with the world, the light is very dim. He is calling us to come up higher and to return to Him for who He is—for truly He is the God of all power and might, and He wants to demonstrate His power over all the earth. However, He has to deal with sin. He is calling us to repentance and to holy living.

He wants to clean up His Church so that He can begin in a greater and greater way to demonstrate His power to the world around us. He is calling His Church to holiness and purity. Will you answer, "Yes, Lord; You may invade my life and my space and purify me with Your cleansing fire so that You can use me the way You desire to use me"? If so, just invite Him and say, "Purify me, Lord, with Your cleansing fire, so that You can bring me forth as pure gold, a vessel of honor in Your house that will not bring reproach on Your Name. Amen."

Wisdom

Who is wise and understanding among you? Let him show by good conduct that his works are done in the meekness of wisdom. But if you have bitter envy and self-seeking in your hearts, do not boast and lie against the truth. This wisdom does not descend from above, but is earthly, sensual, demonic. For where envy and self-seeking exist, confusion and every evil thing are there. But the wisdom that is from above is first pure, then peaceable, gentle, willing to yield, full of mercy and good fruits, without partiality and without hypocrisy (James 3:13–17).

The fear of the LORD is the beginning of wisdom; A good understanding have all those who do His commandments. His praise endures forever (Psalm 111:10).

The fear of the LORD is the beginning of knowledge, But fools despise wisdom and instruction (Proverbs 1:7).

The fear of the LORD is the beginning of wisdom, And the knowledge of the Holy One is understanding (Proverbs 9:10).

This Scripture passage from James contrasts the wisdom that comes from God with earthly wisdom. They are like opposite worlds; what a difference there is in the two! When we examine the difference, it makes earthly wisdom seem more like craftiness than actual wisdom. Godly wisdom is knowing how to apply and live by God's Word and its principles. It is the skill to apply knowledge rightly or righteously. It is impossible to have godly wisdom without knowing God Himself.

God has inspired His Word so that we can find there the wisdom He wants us to have. It says that if we walk in the fear of God it is the beginning of wisdom in our lives. This does not mean that we go through every day of our lives being afraid of what God will do to us. It means that we agree with His Word and we understand the benefits of applying His Word to our lives. We have great reverence and respect for the commandments of Jesus because we understand that not doing so brings consequences, which will take away our joy and peace. We want to live in the blessings of obedience to His Word.

The Bible has those instructions for us and tells us exactly what it means to "fear the Lord." It simply means we hate the things God hates and we do all we can to avoid practicing those things. It says God hates pride, arrogance, and all evil. He wants our conversation to be wholesome so that we will not grieve the Holy Spirit with our words. Words and desires stem from within us, and they are a matter of the heart. Jesus said our mouths speak from the abundance of our hearts (Matthew 12:34). Therefore, the changes begin in our hearts. When we really start to grasp that fact, we are beginning to understand God's wisdom.

Wisdom and knowledge come from understanding the Word of God, the commandments of God, not from just being able to quote some Scripture. We have to have the Spirit of the Word working in us and opening our understanding to how to live and apply the Word of God in our lives and the events in our everyday lives. In addition, when we understand it we can start helping other people to do the same. Second Timothy 2:15 says *"Be diligent to present yourself approved to God, a worker who does not need to be ashamed, rightly dividing the word of truth.*" That means we are to be careful to teach and explain the Word of God correctly and appropriately by accurately discerning its truth. We have to have the Spirit of the Word in order to understand and teach the Word accurately. This is wisdom.

When Solomon became king he recognized that God had shown great mercy to his father, David, when he was king because David walked before God in truth, in righteousness, and in uprightness of heart. Solomon seemed to recognize the great responsibility he himself had before God to do what was right in the eyes of God for the people he would rule over as king. So when God appeared to him in a dream and asked what He should give to Solomon, Solomon said, "*Therefore give to Your servant an understanding heart to judge Your people, that I may discern between good and evil. For who is able to judge this great people of Yours?*" (1 Kings 3:9). That takes the wisdom of God, and Solomon knew that only God could give him that wisdom. We will find it by growing in our relationship with God—that is what knowing Him means. We get to know Him by reading, studying, and meditating on His Word so that we walk with Him.

The knowledge of God understood in our lives opens us up to the wisdom of God. Wisdom is God's truth rightly applied.

The wisdom of God is something we should seek after. There is nothing more valuable than this in all of life. I perceive that many of you are crying out to God and saying, "Oh how I want this wisdom to operate in my life! I long to have godly wisdom like Solomon had, to know what to do when I am in perplexing or difficult times and critical decisions need to be made." First, it does not come from people or a person. It only comes from God Himself, and He has revealed His ways to us in His Word. In order to know Him, we must spend time with Him and we must make His Word the top priority in our daily lives. We all have access to

God the Father through Jesus the Son and Savior, and He will come by His Holy Spirit to live in us. He will lead us, guide us, instruct us, and open our understanding to His Truth.

As we abide in Him and let His Word abide in us, this wisdom will grow in our lives. Remember I said earlier that the wisdom of God is the Word of God rightly applied to life's situations. Where can you find it? You will find it in Him and in His Word. That is where you must go, because you cannot operate in His wisdom without Him.

I will close this with the following Scripture because His Word is the Source of Wisdom:

"I, wisdom, dwell with prudence, And find out knowledge and discretion. The fear of the LORD is to hate evil; Pride and arrogance and the evil way And the perverse mouth I hate. Counsel is mine, and sound wisdom; I am understanding, I have strength. By me kings reign, And rulers decree justice. By me princes rule, and nobles, All the judges of the earth. I love those who love me, And those who seek me diligently will find me. Riches and honor are with me, Enduring riches and righteousness. My fruit is better than gold, yes, than fine gold, And my revenue than choice silver I traverse the way of righteousness, In the midst of the paths of justice, That I may cause those who love me to inherit wealth, That I may fill their treasuries. The LORD possessed me at the beginning of His way, Before His works of old. I have been established from everlasting, From the beginning, before there was ever an earth" (Proverbs 8:12–23).

Authority

And Jesus came and spoke to them, saying, "All authority has been given to Me in heaven and on earth. Go therefore and make disciples of all the nations, baptizing them in the name of the Father and of the Son and of the Holy Spirit, teaching them to observe all things that I have commanded you; and lo, I am with you always, even to the end of the age." Amen (Matthew 28:18–20).

"I am the true vine, and My Father is the vinedresser. Every branch in Me that does not bear fruit He takes away; and every branch that bears fruit He prunes, that it may bear more fruit. You are already clean because of the word which I have spoken to you. Abide in Me, and I in you. As the branch cannot bear fruit of itself, unless it abides in the vine, neither can you, unless you abide in Me. I am the vine, you are the branches. He who abides in Me, and I in him, bears much fruit; for without Me you can do nothing. If anyone does not abide in Me, he is cast out as a branch and is withered; and they gather them and throw them into the fire, and they are burned. If you abide in Me, and My words abide in you, you will ask what you desire, and it shall be done for you. By this My Father is glorified, that you bear much fruit; so you will be My disciples" (John 15:1–8).

After Jesus' crucifixion and resurrection from the dead, He had fully accomplished the Father's will, and that qualified Him to have all rule and authority in heaven and earth. He stayed on earth long enough to show Himself to His own, who would be witnesses to His resurrection, and some other people too. He gave His disciples some final instructions as to what they needed to do to fulfill their mission on this earth. He accomplished His own mission, and He was returning to the Father who sent Him to earth for His divine purpose.

We read about a centurion in Matthew 8:5-10 who turned to Jesus for help when his servant was lying at home paralyzed and dreadfully tormented. He told Jesus that He did not need to go to his house to heal the servant; all He needed to do was speak the word, and it would be accomplished. He said this because he understood the authority Jesus had over that realm.

The centurion had a good understanding of authority, and he demonstrated that when he told Jesus that he too was a man *"under authority,"* having soldiers under him. He told Jesus that he understood authority because he too had authority. When he told someone to go, he went; when he told another to come, he came; and when he told another soldier to do something, he did it. Likewise, he understood the authority Jesus had from heaven, that all Jesus needed to do was speak the orders and everything, including sickness and paralysis and torment, had to obey Him.

As believers, we have authority as long as we remain under authority. God gives it to us as long as we abide in Him. It flows through believers. In order for us as believers to be walking in authority, we have to be hearing from the One who has authority over us. Authority flows from the top down, and everyone in authority must be under someone else's authority first. Jesus told us that His Father has given all authority to Him. He also said that He, the Son of God, can do nothing of Himself, but only what He sees the Father doing, and then He does whatever He sees Him doing (John 5:19). In John 5:30 Jesus said, *"I can of Myself do nothing. As I hear, I judge; and My judgment is righteous, because I do not seek My own will but the will of the Father who sent Me."*

As New Testament believers, we all have the Holy Spirit to teach us, lead us and guide us in our daily lives. He convicts us of sin, opens our understanding to what is right and what is wrong in His eyes, and orders the steps of the righteous. He teaches us truth. He bears witness that we are the children of God. When we have the life of the Holy Spirit in us, we can also walk in the Spirit (Galatians 5:25).

God has also set up authority in His church. We have the Holy Spirit to teach us and train us and lead us every day, but that does not mean it is a good idea to be islands unto ourselves. We need to fellowship with other believers. It is for our protection. Moreover, we are stronger as a group of people who fellowship together than we are on our own without being connected to a fellowship of other believers.

Church leaders are not there to carry out their own desires and ambitions. They are not there to get the people to do their will, but they are to find out and carry out the will of the One whose authority they are to submit to first. As they operate under authority, they are there to lead the people into what the Head of the Church, Christ, wants them to do. We are to follow them as they follow Christ. That is very different from simply obeying a leader. We are not to obey the leader, but we are to follow the leaders as they follow Christ.

This does not mean we do not hear from God individually, but it does mean God also has a bigger plan than just the individual knowing Him. God does want us to know Him intimately, and as we all develop and grow in that relationship the entire church will mature.

Some leaders have abused authority in the church. They have wounded many people because of their misuse of authority. Many people who are professing Christians no longer attend a local church because of the abuses and are disillusioned and very reluctant to attend church anymore. That is tragic and certainly not the plan of God. If the leaders were following the plan of the One who is the Head and under whose authority they are to operate, these abuses would not happen.

The Kingdom of God rules on earth as the believers yield to the Holy Spirit, and He rules through the freedom people allow Him as they obey Him and walk in the Spirit. For us to receive the orders we must listen for His voice and then be quick to do what He says. God does not want leaders to build individual kingdoms or empires, but He wants them to shepherd the people, nurture them, show them by example how to live as Christians, and let them develop their relationships with God and not interfere with that growth and development that only the Holy Spirit can bring about.

In Acts 20:28–31 Paul the Apostle in his exhortation to the elders at Ephesus said this:

> *"Therefore take heed to yourselves and to all the flock, among which the Holy Spirit has made you overseers, to shepherd the church of God which He purchased with His own blood. For I know this, that after my departure savage wolves will come in among you, not sparing the flock. Also from among yourselves men will rise up, speaking perverse things, to draw away the disciples after themselves. Therefore watch, and remember that for three years I did not cease to warn everyone night and day with tears."*

Just as Paul warned the people that after he left wolves would rise up among them, so it happens amongst God's people today.

The fruit coming from their lives gives them away (Matthew 7:15–20). God wants loving leaders in the Church who will submit to Him in humility and the fear of God.

I sense from the Holy Spirit that some of you have wounds. God wants to restore you. You have seen a lot in the Church that does not reflect the heart of God our Father; consequently, you have become very fearful of being a part of a congregation. However, God wants to heal you of the wounds. He is the loving Shepherd who heals us and restores us and strengthens us.

Let Him heal you today if you are hurting, and ask Him to lead you back into a congregation if you are not a part of one at this time. He has a place for you to find fellowship with other believers, and He is not condemning you, but He wants to heal you.

Ask God to give you revelation about His authority in your life, and let Him teach you what it really means. He will teach you in His kind and loving way, and He will bring peace and contentment into your life. He knows how to settle in our hearts the things we have struggled with in the past. He gives understanding through His Word.

The Lord, the Shepherd, Restores Our Souls

The LORD is my shepherd; I shall not want. He makes me to lie down in green pastures; He leads me beside the still waters. He restores my soul; He leads me in the paths of righteousness For His name's sake. Yea, though I walk through the valley of the shadow of death, I will fear no evil; For You are with me; Your rod and Your staff, they comfort me. You prepare a table before me in the presence of my enemies; You anoint my head with oil; My cup runs over. Surely goodness and mercy shall follow me All the days of my life; And I will dwell in the house of the LORD Forever (Psalm 23:1–6).

The Good Shepherd will restore our souls. That means He wants to bring us back to the way He always intended us to be, including health and general well-being for the whole person. The most common definition of the soul is our mind, emotions, and will.

When we come into the fold of the Good Shepherd and we are born anew of God's Spirit, the Holy Spirit begins to work in us to change us into the person God wants us to become. We do not become someone else, but we become a brand new creation in Christ. God's will is for us to become like Christ in nature. In that process we are being transformed into the person God sees. Galatians 4:19 says, "*My little children, for whom I labor in birth again until Christ is formed in you.*" Paul the Apostle refers to this development in us as "*Christ [being] formed in you*" (Galatians 4:19).

God works in us to bring out His best in each of us. He irons out the wrinkles and removes the flaws in our character. This is His work in us to bring us to maturity as children of God. Philippians 2:13 says, "*For it is God who works in you both to will and to do for His good pleasure.*" He is continually working in us by His Spirit and bringing us to maturity in character so that we will be like Christ in character and desire. There is a profound change in the heart of people so that they become like Jesus in nature. God is continually transforming them into His likeness, as it says in 2 Corinthians 3:18: "*But we all, with unveiled face, beholding as in a mirror the glory of the Lord, are being transformed into the same image from glory to glory, just as by the Spirit of the Lord.*"

Individuals come to know the Lord Jesus from all kinds of backgrounds, having had many different experiences. Some people need more restoration from past wounds than others, but we all need some work done in us. God begins that work as soon as we turn our lives over to Him. We are definitely children of God from the moment we are born again, but we are not mature Christians at that moment. That is just the beginning of the new life we have in Christ Jesus. The carnal, or old, nature has to die daily, and the new nature of the Holy Spirit must replace it.

When we understand that God is working in us, it will make it less frustrating and even less confusing when God allows us to go through many of the things that He will. Even Jesus learned obedience to the Father by the things He suffered. Hebrews 5:8 says, "*Though He was a Son, yet He learned obedience by the things which He suffered.*" When we suffer, we too have to yield to the will of the Father and discipline our own wills to bow to His so that we learn what we need to from the experiences God will use in our lives to bring us to maturity.

As we grow in intimacy with God and we let the Shepherd restore our souls, we become mature in the things of God. In order for this work to happen the way God wants it to in us, we need to spend time with Him and read and meditate on His Word. As we do this, our understanding will be opened more and more to God's Word and how to apply it to our own lives on a daily basis.

The Word and the Spirit of God work together in us. With the Word, our minds become renewed, and the Holy Spirit gives us understanding and produces Holy Spirit fruit in our lives. Having the mind of Christ is simply coming into agreement with the way He thinks. We find that out by understanding His Word.

The transformation process is a lifelong journey. It is the Spirit of God working in us, but we can certainly cooperate and make it much more enjoyable, or at least more rewarding, to experience this growth by looking forward to what God is doing in us, instead of resisting that because we do not understand. The more we cooperate, the quicker we mature.

If we yield to His leading, He will satisfy us by causing us to lie down or find perfect provision in tender green pastures where He feeds us well. He will lead us beside still waters of peace. He makes us whole and His presence will bring everything we need for life. His mercy will follow us throughout our lives. He will keep us in the paths of righteousness for His own honor and glory. We will dwell with Him for eternity.

Just ask the Lord to lead you on this journey and to enrich your spiritual walk by taking you to these "secret places" in Him, and you will find out that He is very eager to answer that prayer. God bless you.

Loneliness

Now in the morning, having risen a long while before daylight, He went out and departed to a solitary place; and there He prayed (Mark 1:35).

Coming out, He went to the Mount of Olives, as He was accustomed, and His disciples also followed Him. When He came to the place, He said to them, "Pray that you may not enter into temptation." And He was withdrawn from them about a stone's throw, and He knelt down and prayed, saying, "Father, if it is Your will, take this cup away from Me; nevertheless not My will, but Yours, be done." Then an angel appeared to Him from heaven, strengthening Him. And being in agony, He prayed more earnestly. Then His sweat became like great drops of blood falling down to the ground. When He rose up from prayer, and had come to His disciples, He found them sleeping from sorrow. Then He said to them, "Why do you sleep? Rise and pray, lest you enter into temptation" (Luke 22:39–46).

Now it came to pass in those days that He went out to the mountain to pray, and continued all night in prayer to God. And when it was day, He called His disciples to Himself; and from them He chose twelve whom He also named apostles: Simon, whom He also named Peter, and Andrew his brother;

> *James and John; Philip and Bartholomew; Matthew and Thomas; James the son of Alphaeus, and Simon called the Zealot; Judas the son of James, and Judas Iscariot who also became a traitor. And He came down with them and stood on a level place with a crowd of His disciples and a great multitude of people from all Judea and Jerusalem, and from the seacoast of Tyre and Sidon, who came to hear Him and be healed of their diseases, as well as those who were tormented with unclean spirits. And they were healed. And the whole multitude sought to touch Him, for power went out from Him and healed them all* (Luke 6:12–19).

From these Scriptures it is clear that Jesus spent extended times with the Father alone. He went to solitary places and sought the Father's face. He often separated Himself from the crowds and even His own disciples while He went away alone to commune with His Father.

Sometimes it was after He had ministered to huge crowds, and sometimes it was before He made very important decisions and He wanted to know His Father's heart and obey in all things. Before He chose the twelve apostles, He spent an entire night alone in prayer. After He chose the twelve, following His night in prayer, a great multitude of people gathered around Him to hear Him preach and to be healed of their diseases. He healed them all. Those tormented with unclean spirits were set free from the devil's power over their lives.

It is obvious from the Scripture passages that Jesus experienced loneliness. When He sought the Father's face, for entire nights or long hours early in the morning, with anguish and earnest prayer in order to hear the Father's voice and do His will in all things, He must have experienced loneliness.

Compared with what Jesus had to experience, the things we experience are small; on a lesser scale we too will go through similar sufferings to learn obedience. Hebrews 5:8 says that even though Jesus was God's Son He still learned obedience by the things He suffered. If we are going to draw close to the Father and learn to hear His voice and experience that communion with Him, we too will go through times of loneliness—maybe even intense loneliness.

These are times when we cannot get our answers from a book or from another Christian. We too are in a place of solitude with God during such times. Sometimes we cannot see very far ahead or know exactly what God is doing in us or His purpose for it. God allows those things in our lives, and sometimes, by divine design, He weaves those times into the journey of our lives so that we can become more like Jesus.

The loneliness can be very difficult. Perhaps we wonder what is wrong with us at those times. We wait and we long for someone to come along who understands exactly what is happening to us, but God will not allow it. He will keep us there until He is finished with us and until it has done the work in us that He wants it to do.

God wants us to learn to trust Him and follow Him, even when no one else does. During these lonely times, we may feel rejected and even feel as though God has left us alone, and yet He promised never to leave us or forsake us. However, sometimes it feels as though He has.

Sometimes when God speaks to us and is asking things of us that He is not asking of those around us, we will experience rejection, misunderstanding, and criticism from those who do not understand. Then we must answer the question God is asking: "Will you be My disciple?" This means we will not be following the crowd, and maybe the crowd will not like us very much for a while, but God is testing us to see if we will still follow Him.

This is quite a wilderness experience! However, if we yield to Him while in the wilderness, it will produce the kind of fruit in our lives that reflects His own Son, Jesus, and that is the purpose.

To those who are going through a wilderness experience, God is saying do not despair. Though you feel as though this will never end, it will end, and you will feel different when it is over than you think you will. The things that were important to you before will be far less important after you come out of the wilderness after your test. Your priorities will change, because your heart will change. You will begin more and more to see things that truly matter for eternity rather than for just here and now.

When the furnace seems hot, keep calling out to God, and He will strengthen you from on high so that you will come through and come forth as purified gold. You will experience a deeper peace and rest than you knew before, and it will not be so dependent on your circumstances.

Fear

There is no fear in love; but perfect love casts out fear, because fear involves torment. But he who fears has not been made perfect in love (1 John 4:18).

For God has not given us a spirit of fear, but of power and of love and of a sound mind (2 Timothy 1:7).

With the merciful You will show Yourself merciful; With a blameless man You will show Yourself blameless; With the pure You will show Yourself pure; And with the devious You will show Yourself shrewd. You will save the humble people But will bring down haughty looks. For You will light my lamp; The LORD my God will enlighten my darkness. For by You I can run against a troop, By my God I can leap over a wall. As for God, His way is perfect; The word of the LORD is proven; He is a shield to all who trust in Him. For who is God, except the LORD? And who is a rock, except our God? It is God who arms me with strength, And makes my way perfect. He makes my feet like the feet of deer, And sets me on my high places. He teaches my hands to make war, So that my arms can bend a bow of bronze. You have also given me the shield of Your salvation; Your right hand has held me up, Your gentleness has made me great. You enlarged my path under me, So my feet did not slip (Psalm 18:25–36).

Many times the Bible tells us not to fear. Moreover, the only one we should fear is God. In Matthew 10:28 Jesus said, "*And do not fear those who kill the body but cannot kill the soul. But rather fear Him who is able to destroy both soul and body in hell.*"

When we fear only God, we stay focused on Him and His word. We pay close attention to what He has to say to us in our everyday living. When we focus on Him and His Word, we are abiding in the secret place. There He keeps us safe from many of the things that we fear in the natural. The fear of God causes us to take Him seriously and do what He says, because we understand that anything else is disobedience to Him, and that will eventually bring some negative consequences. If we keep God at the forefront of our minds in all we do, we are becoming wise in the most fundamental aspect of this life.

We feed and strengthen what we focus on the most. Fear can eventually consume us if we do not discipline ourselves and take control of our thoughts. This fear can get to the point where it almost paralyzes us from making decisions. There are innumerable fears if we allow ourselves to dwell on them. Often we fear people, and we wonder what they will think of us if we do certain things. We wonder what they will say about us, what if this happens, or what if that happens. We fear rejection, and we wonder if God will really see us through our difficulties. Is He really watching over us, and can He really be trusted? Our focus feeds our fears instead of removing them from us. What we focus on the most is what will drive us, and the more we focus on it, the stronger it becomes in our lives. We empower it by giving it excessive space in our minds by allowing the "what if" thoughts to roam freely and at will.

So then what should we do? First John 4:18 says perfect love casts out fear. Perfect love is mature love, and that is God's love. When we focus on God and His Word and meditate on that, we are feeding on the very things that transform us into His nature, and then the confidence that He can be trusted grows in our hearts. His Word renews our minds, and this is transformation. This is how we mature as a Christian, and the more we mature, the less we fear other things in life.

We know that He has promised never to leave us nor forsake us, and that is the promise in Hebrews 13:5. He is with us forever. He is Immanuel, God with us. He is *"Wonderful, Counselor, Mighty God, Everlasting Father, Prince of Peace"* (Isaiah 9:6). Our confidence in God, knowing who He is and that He is always with us, replaces negative fear and drives it out of our lives.

In Joshua chapter 1, we read God's words to Joshua after Moses died and Joshua was chosen to take the people across the Jordan and into the Promised Land. Several times God spoke to Joshua to get him to focus on God and His Word and not to fear the way things looked and the things they would face on the journey.

In verses 6 to 9 God spoke to Joshua, saying,

> *"Be strong and of good courage, for to this people you shall divide as an inheritance the land which I swore to their fathers to give them. Only be strong and very courageous, that you may observe to do according to all the law which Moses My servant commanded you; do not turn from it to the right hand or to the left, that you may prosper wherever you go. This Book of the Law shall not depart from your mouth, but you shall meditate in it day and night, that you may observe to do according to all that is written in it. For then you will make your way prosperous, and then you will have good success. Have I not commanded you? Be strong and of good courage; do not be afraid, nor be dismayed, for the LORD your God is with you wherever you go."*

The Lord reminded Joshua repeatedly that he was not to fear. God told him to fear not and to be of good courage and to just obey. Courage does not mean that we do not "feel" fear but that we do what we know is right in spite of the fear. This is how we overcome our fears and how our confidence in God's faithfulness and protection increases in our lives.

If we succumb to fear of all the possible things that might happen to us if we step out in faith, we will never get beyond those fears. They will control or immobilize us. Trusting God helps us to do what we should be doing even when we feel afraid. We choose, then, to agree with God and His Word, and then faith rises up in our hearts, the weak, knocking knees are strengthened, and the hands that hang down are lifted up in victory.

The most detrimental thing we can do is dwell on our fears. All the "what ifs" keep many people from doing great things. They choose to stay safe because they are so afraid of failure.

What if we make a mistake or we are wrong or we do not succeed? We all ask ourselves these questions when new challenges open up to us. We all make mistakes. When we do fail at something, all that really matters is that we learn from those mistakes and grow in wisdom because of them. We ask the question, What if I fail? However, what about the alternative: What if I succeed? If we allow these fears to hinder us, we will never discover what we are capable of doing, because we allow the fear to keep us from trying anything we have not done before.

Fear is a favorite weapon Satan uses against us. We have to choose to act with courage and say no to fear. Second Timothy 1:7 says, *"God has not given us a spirit of fear, but of power and of love and of a sound mind."* God has given us His Spirit, and that means we have good judgment. God has given us what we need to equip us to do the things He calls us to do and the things we need to do. We do not have to go around timidly fearing failure all the time and expecting the worst, but we can move ahead with courage when God tells us to step out in faith. His Word makes it very clear that if we do what He asks us to do, He will be with us and we do not need to fear.

There are innumerable fears that we could mention, such as fear of being alone, fear of the dark, fear of man, fear of heights, fear of old age, fear of sickness, fear of death, and fear of the future. Though we cannot possibly name them all, we can overcome them all with God's help and God's Word. The Word of God is full of comfort and hope. We may not know the future and what it holds for each of us, but we know who holds our hand.

Just reading the Word of God brings comfort to us and calms our fears. When we put it into our hearts, we have the armor of God on the inside. We are putting on the armor God has given us. His Spirit living in us has no fear. When we focus on what He says to us and read His Word aloud, it does amazing things to us. When we focus there and meditate on what He says to us and speak it out, we appropriate, or draw to ourselves, the very power it has promised us.

God did not tell Joshua *"do not be afraid"* because there would not be anything to fear. He told Joshua to act with courage because there were going to be many obstacles to overcome. However, God gave him the antidote to the fear, and that was to meditate day and night on the Word of the Lord and not to give way to fear but to proceed with courage. Then the fear would leave. When God asks us to do something and we act upon that, He backs us up with His power, and His presence goes with us. He does not leave us alone.

In Joshua 1:9 the Lord instructed Joshua, saying, *"Be strong and of good courage; do not be afraid, nor be dismayed, for the LORD your God is with you wherever you go."* Take heart; that is true for you and me as well. If God asks us to do something, we do not need to be afraid, because He is with us as He has promised. We overcome our fears by facing them head-on. It takes faith to step out and do that. However, when we do, our faith grows.

Uncertainty

To everything there is a season, A time for every purpose under heaven: A time to be born, And a time to die; A time to plant, And a time to pluck what is planted; A time to kill, And a time to heal; A time to break down, And a time to build up; A time to weep, And a time to laugh; A time to mourn, And a time to dance; A time to cast away stones, And a time to gather stones; A time to embrace, And a time to refrain from embracing; A time to gain, And a time to lose; A time to keep, And a time to throw away; A time to tear, And a time to sew; A time to keep silence, And a time to speak; A time to love, And a time to hate; A time of war, And a time of peace (Ecclesiastes 3:1–8).

Sometimes we go through seasons when we do not see anything clearly. It is as though we are walking through fog all the time. We want it to lift so that we can clearly see what God is accomplishing in our lives, but nothing seems clear.

What do these things do in us? It is just one more way God keeps us close to Him. Sometimes we think we hear God's voice, and then things get tough and we start to wonder if we really did hear His voice. If we did, then why is it so difficult? Why is it so strange at times? Why does it seem so uncertain? I remember many times of uncertainty when I cried out to God and said, "Please verify the things that I have thought You said so that I will know what You want me to cling to, what You want me to keep believing. And if it was not really Your voice I heard, then just tell me." Often it just went on and on and on, and there was no sign from God that I had not heard from Him but there was also no new confirmation that I had.

Those are times when we just have to trust God and walk in the faith that we have in Him, who has promised to lead us and keep our feet from slipping so that we will be kept on the path of righteousness that He put us on to begin with. These are not easy times, but they sure do teach us to trust Him. He does want us to trust Him so that we will not fear even when we cannot see very far ahead, but we will hold on to His invisible hand and keep moving ahead.

The things we are waiting for and hoping for in these uncertain times are the things we have perceived in our spirits but have not yet seen with our natural eyes. Our spirits have grasped what God is saying, and we feel a pull in that direction. Our souls longs to understand it all, and our flesh does not like the uncertainty one bit. It is when we pursue what the Spirit of God has put inside of us that we are learning to obey the Spirit, or walk in the Spirit. As it says in Galatians 5:25, "*If we live in the Spirit, let us also walk in the Spirit.*" That means we follow what the Holy Spirit is convicting us to do even if it makes no sense to our reasoning at the time. If and when the Holy Spirit speaks, He will never contradict God's inspired Word. They are always in agreement.

Uncertainty means that nothing is sure. We want to know, but we do not know. We search and we long for answers and direction, but everything seems vague and invisible. Other than what the Spirit of God is saying to us on the inside of us, in our spirits, we just do not know. All these things help us to die to the flesh. Paul said in 1 Corinthians 15:31, "*I affirm, by the boasting in you which I have in Christ Jesus our Lord, I die daily.*"

Paul also said in Galatians 2:20, "*I have been crucified with Christ; it is no longer I who live, but Christ lives in me; and the life which I now live in the flesh I live by faith in the Son of God, who loved me and gave Himself for me.*" We now have to understand that Christ died for us, and by the grace of God we now have the Spirit of God living in us as Christians to enable us to let Christ live through us, and we do this by faith.

These things are very frustrating to our flesh or natural man, but God takes us through these experiences so that we will learn to walk in faith and so the invisible will become more real to us than the visible. Once we can see the answer, we don't need any faith; but when we cannot see the answer and we are even uncertain that there is an answer, then we really need to trust and walk in faith.

"*Now faith is the substance of things hoped for, the evidence of things not seen*" (Hebrews 11:1). "*The substance of things hoped for*" means the realization of things hoped for, and "*the evidence of things not see*n" means the confidence we have in those things we do not yet see. We can only receive that from God's Word and the Holy Spirit giving us that assurance as He lives in us.

Heavenly Father,

Help me to see through the eyes of faith when there is nothing visible to cling to, and teach me how to keep following You in times of uncertainty. When I cannot see what lies ahead, make Your voice the clearest voice to me. Strengthen me to do Your will and to obey Your Word, even when everything else seems uncertain to me. Do not let me wander off the path that You have set before me, but guide me with Your hand on the paths of righteousness for Your Name's sake as You promised in Psalm 23. In Jesus' name I ask, and I thank You for hearing me. Amen.

Dread

And whatever you do, do it heartily, as to the Lord and not to men, knowing that from the Lord you will receive the reward of the inheritance; for you serve the Lord Christ (Colossians 3:23–24).

Rejoice always, pray without ceasing, in everything give thanks; for this is the will of God in Christ Jesus for you (1 Thessalonians 5:16–18).

Be anxious for nothing, but in everything by prayer and supplication, with thanksgiving, let your requests be made known to God; and the peace of God, which surpasses all understanding, will guard your hearts and minds through Christ Jesus. Finally, brethren, whatever things are true, whatever things are noble, whatever things are just, whatever things are pure, whatever things are lovely, whatever things are of good report, if there is any virtue and if there is anything praiseworthy—meditate on these things (Philippians 4:6–8).

My first thought today as I begin this writing is that I dread getting started. How do I tell someone else what dread is like and what its purpose is in life? It seems that we need things to look forward to, because that is what gives us an incentive to keep doing the things that we have to do but really dread doing. When we discipline ourselves to face the things we dread and do them anyway, knowing they are the right thing to do, it often helps us to get to the things we want to do and the things we look forward to doing. We all have to exercise discipline in our personal lives so that we do not become procrastinators, giving way to our feelings and avoiding doing the things we dread. Overcoming the things we dread is the same as overcoming fear. We overcome dread when we do what we know we need to do, in spite of the dread. After we complete the dreaded task, we feel a sense of relief and satisfaction. Instead of feeling stressed and guilty because we are procrastinating, we have a sense of God's peace. This is how we get rid of dread. We just face it, do it, and then get on with things we actually do not mind doing or look forward to doing.

Sometimes we dread facing a situation or a person from whom we may receive some discipline or correction that we feel is coming our way, and so we do our best to avoid it, because we dread it. We dread the things we fear, the things that cause us anxiety, and situations where we fear the outcome, not knowing what awaits us…and on and on it goes. We sometimes dread meeting new people because we do not know if they will like us or if we will be able to get along with them. Sometimes we have to start a new job, and that can be stressful. We do not know anyone, and we barely even know the person who will be our supervisor or boss. Maybe we have only met them once at the job interview. These things are necessities of life but things we may dread. We cannot avoid all of the things we dread. Therefore, we move ahead in faith, believing that God will help us and the Holy Spirit will guide us, and They do.

Why would God allow us to experience these things? They are all a part of character development and learning to walk by faith and believing for the best. Sometimes I do not feel like cleaning the house or planning the meals or washing the windows or shoveling the walk after it snows, but if I sit here and dread them and do not do anything about it, I will not overcome them. If by the end of the day I still have not cleaned the house, I will feel worse. If I have not done the things I should have done, just because they were things I do not like and I dreaded them, I will keep feeling worse until I finally get them done. Then I will have to wake up again the next day and dread the same things.

However, if I get out the vacuum cleaner, vacuum the floors, wash them, and do the dusting, and everything is nice and clean, the very thing I dreaded and now have accomplished will give me a sense of satisfaction. I look forward to the clean house, not the housework. The goal motivates me, and that is why I do the things I dread. We need to keep our eyes on the goal and not on the things we dread, and that is an incentive to do them anyway. We will not feel good about things we avoid and procrastinate in doing, but we do experience rest, peace, and satisfaction when we discipline ourselves to do mundane things and things we dread or even fear, even if no one other than God sees that we did them.

Avoidance is not a good thing. It keeps us from experiencing God's peace. There are certain things in life that we all have to do, and some of them are things we dread. When we discipline ourselves to do them, we enjoy more rest and peace. Avoiding things we do not look forward to and the tactics we use to do that will drain us of our energy, but facing the mountain head-on and asking God to take us to the top of it will deliver us from procrastination and give us peace. It is a peaceful and rewarding feeling to have faced something we dreaded and then to have the reward of God's peace, knowing that we have done what He would have us do.

There must have been things Jesus dreaded when He was fulfilling His mission on earth. Imagine what it must have been like to look forward to the cross. Hebrews 12:1–2 says,

> *Therefore we also, since we are surrounded by so great a cloud of witnesses, let us lay aside every weight, and the sin which so*

easily ensnares us, and let us run with endurance the race that is set before us, looking unto Jesus, the author and finisher of our faith, who for the joy that was set before Him endured the cross, despising the shame, and has sat down at the right hand of the throne of God.

Jesus predicted His own death on the cross, and He said this in John 12:27–28:

"Now My soul has become troubled; and what shall I say, 'Father, save Me from this hour'? But for this purpose I came to this hour. Father, glorify Your name." Then a voice came out of heaven: "I have both glorified it, and will glorify it again."

Heavenly Father,

We ask today for a thankful heart. Help us to remember to thank You and praise You for all You do and all You are. We will rejoice and give You thanks today. It is the day that You have made.

Help us to keep our eyes on the goal You set before us so that we will not focus on the mundane and the negative but keep our eyes fixed on Jesus, who is the author and finisher of or faith.

Give us the courage we need to overcome the things we dread so that we can face You with confidence and say what Paul said in 2 Timothy 4:7–8: "*I have fought the good fight, I have finished the race, I have kept the faith. Finally, there is laid up for me the crown of righteousness, which the Lord, the righteous Judge, will give to me on that Day, and not to me only but also to all who have loved His appearing.*"
In Jesus' name we ask, and we thank You. Amen.

Physical Pain

Who has believed our report? And to whom has the arm of the LORD been revealed? For He shall grow up before Him as a tender plant, And as a root out of dry ground. He has no form or comeliness; And when we see Him, There is no beauty that we should desire Him. He is despised and rejected by men, A Man of sorrows and acquainted with grief. And we hid, as it were, our faces from Him; He was despised, and we did not esteem Him. Surely He has borne our griefs And carried our sorrows; Yet we esteemed Him stricken, Smitten by God, and afflicted. But He was wounded for our transgressions, He was bruised for our iniquities; The chastisement for our peace was upon Him, And by His stripes we are healed (Isaiah 53:1–5).

Bless the LORD, O my soul; And all that is within me, bless His holy name! Bless the LORD, O my soul, And forget not all His benefits: Who forgives all your iniquities, Who heals all your diseases, Who redeems your life from destruction, Who crowns you with lovingkindness and tender mercies, Who satisfies your mouth with good things, So that your youth is renewed like the eagle's (Psalm 103:1–5).

Why do we experience physical pain when it is clear in the Bible that Jesus is our healer and that He took upon Himself all sickness and disease as well as our sin when He suffered on the cross and then rose again to give us resurrection life?

That is a huge question. I wish I could provide all the answers, but only God has them. It says also that we are appointed once to die (Hebrews 9:27), physical death, so that we can exit from this life to move into eternity, where our bodies are going to be immortal instead of mortal. The mortal body is subject to decay, but the resurrected body will not be subject to decay.

We are not just physical beings. We are spirit, soul, and body. Each part of us affects the others. A person who is suffering great emotional pain may eventually manifest that pain by the body showing it in a physical way. The pain on the inside shows up on the outside, and the person is physically not well.

I am no doctor, and this is not an attempt to try to explain all the things medicine has discovered through research, but it has become common knowledge that stress is a root cause of many physical illnesses. Stress prevents the organs in our body from functioning the way God created them to function. When that happens over long periods, the immune system is weakened. Genetic factors can make us more susceptible to certain diseases, and there are many other things involved that I certainly cannot explain. But we do have some control over what happens to our health and can take steps such as eating right, exercising in a reasonable manner as we are able, getting regular medical checkups, and listening to and actually applying good advice doctors give to us.

It will greatly contribute to our general well-being, including our physical health, when our hearts and minds are at peace. When terrible things happen to people that they don't have control over, it causes great emotional distress. The only way to find release from this is to release those who have caused it. If we cannot or will not forgive others and we carry the things in our souls that wounded us, we will eventually also manifest them in our physical bodies.

Rehashing wrongs or perceived wrongs done to us and refusing to forgive will cause us mental torment and emotional anguish, and both are deadly.

We have to deal with those things. Sometimes the root of an illness can be something other than what is manifested with physical pain. The root can be guilt or shame or condemnation we never got free of from something that happened years ago. Or maybe we just have not been able to forgive the person or persons who were responsible. Often people just need to recognize the root problem and then deal with it in a scriptural manner. Then the physical body will respond to what has happened in the soul by recovering from the physical sickness that had its origin in the soul.

We all face major disappointments in life that we just cannot get over. We blame ourselves, or we blame someone else. We suffer and live in continual remorse, and it is not helping us or anyone else. However, it keeps us from enjoying the present and the future. These are times when our hopes are dashed, and it is hard to get over it and move on again with hope. When our hope is gone or delayed it is very difficult to have a positive outlook. As it says in Proverbs 13:12, *"Hope deferred makes the heart sick, But when the desire comes, it is a tree of life."*

When we are under stress that we cannot eliminate, how can we take responsibility for the stress-related health problems and avoid them? We can spend time with God regularly, read His Word, and listen carefully to what He is telling us. This alone is one very effective way to unload our cares, release our stress, and find solace in Him. It may not take away the stressful situations, but it will definitely help us to cope and experience less stress. Reading the Bible and asking God to help us apply it as much as we are capable of doing to our personal lives and the stressful situations that truly are beyond our control will help us on a daily basis. We cannot avoid all stress. However, we can minimize its effect on our mental and emotional health, which eventually affect our physical health, by doing what we can about it.

We need to do our best with God's help to plan our days and allow time to just sit and relax, listen to what God is telling us, and eliminate things that are not essential. Our lives should not be so busy that we cannot rest and experience God's peace in the midst of our stress. This takes focus and planning and conscious concerted effort to start making changes that will help us in the end.

No matter what I have to face, it is always a lot easier if I have had a proper night's sleep. Relaxing before I go to bed, winding down from the busyness, and doing something that is conducive to peaceful sleep is one way I do it. I do not like to listen to the news on television late at night, because often it is very negative and even disturbing, and those are not the last things I want on my mind before I go to bed. I have found it helpful if I read something before I go to bed that is going to make me think about good things. Sometimes I remind myself of all the blessings I have in life and count the blessings instead of my woes. These practical things help put my mind at ease so that I will rest better through the night. Then when morning comes, it will be easier to handle the stressful things I cannot eliminate from my life. We are all capable of doing these kinds of things so that we take responsibility for our health as much as possible.

Over the years, I have often asked God to tell me and to reveal to His Church why we do not see as many physical healings and creative miracles as they did in the early Church. Many books are available about this subject and certain explanations are given, but they do not seem to satisfy us, because they do not produce the answers we are waiting for. I am still waiting for God to grant me some miracles in the area of physical healing. I have a condition that causes me physical pain every day of my life. I have waited for years for the Lord to heal me, and I have not experienced it so far.

There are times when it seems to be getting much better, and then suddenly the pain escalates again.

However, I have not given up. I still believe the Bible, and I know that Jesus is the healer and that the Holy Spirit's gifts or manifestations include healings and miracles. Therefore, that is what I believe for, even though I have not experienced it yet in my own body.

The pain has many times brought me to God and kept me seeking Him. On days when it is very bad, it often causes depression and hopelessness. On good days, my spirits are up, and then I feel confident again that one day my miracle will be manifested. Also then, my mind feels more peaceful, and my hope is strong again that one day it will leave and never return.

We may have our good days and our bad days when we have pain. There are times when we are more hopeful and times when we are very disappointed and even fearful. Though that part of our lives is subjective to our circumstances, the God of all hope never changes. In addition, that means He is still the healer today.

We know that God is doing those things today, we hear of it, and in some parts of the world it is certainly happening. We know God has not changed, and so we wait for His answers to our longings. Regardless of what caused our sickness, disease, and pain, we now need healing, and we put our trust in God daily to bring that about.

Heavenly Father,

We come to You who are God Almighty. You are the God who does not change. You are forever the same, as it says in Hebrews 13:8, *"Jesus Christ is the same yesterday, today, and forever."* We know and we believe that by the stripes Jesus bore in His body on the cross, we were healed. We ask for understanding about physical healing and that You will heal all those who need physical healing as they read this book.

"*Be diligent to present yourself approved to God, a worker who does not need to be ashamed, rightly dividing the word of truth*" (2 Timothy 2:15). I ask, Heavenly Father, that You would open the eyes of our understanding so that we may rightly divide, teach, and preach Your Word without adding or taking anything away from it.

In Jesus' name we approach Your throne to find mercy in our time of need. Amen.

Weariness

And let us not grow weary while doing good, for in due season we shall reap if we do not lose heart (Galatians 6:9).

Have you not known? Have you not heard? The everlasting God, the LORD, The Creator of the ends of the earth, Neither faints nor is weary. His understanding is unsearchable. He gives power to the weak, And to those who have no might He increases strength. Even the youths shall faint and be weary, And the young men shall utterly fall, But those who wait on the LORD Shall renew their strength; They shall mount up with wings like eagles, They shall run and not be weary, They shall walk and not faint (Isaiah 40:28–31).

In the presence of God, our strength is renewed. When we wait on God He replenishes what has been taken from us through the toil of the day, the routine tasks we do out of necessity, and the unexpected events that come into our lives that take our time, energy, and attention.

We enter into rest and we are refreshed when we wait in the presence of God. If we go on day after day without it, we may become very weary with life. There are daily necessities that the things that are normal and right for each one of us to do require of us. Though we cannot avoid them, they still make us tired and perhaps very bored with our daily routines. We all get weary from these things at one time or another. If we do not make time to find refreshing in God's presence, drawing from the river of God within us—God's Holy Spirit, who revives us and helps us to keep our eyes focused on Him—we can easily become very discouraged with doing good, because we do not see the rewards at the time.

Sometimes we can look around and wonder if there is any good reason to keep doing the things we once thought were God's direction for us, because it seems as though no one really cares. However, when we do well, God sees, and God rewards everything that we do unto Him.

Mothers who stay home and raise their children often work very hard all the time, and they do a very noble job. They care in a loving way for their children, and their job is there seven days a week, fifty-two weeks of the year. Often it seems that every day is the same, and you wonder if anyone really notices how hard you work and how diligently you serve the Lord and care for your family and take care of the house. Rest assured God sees all of that and that He will reward you in the right season. While you are doing that, you are sowing toward that reward every single day.

We all need encouragement, and we should make an effort to encourage one another. Let us read Galatians 6:10: "*Therefore, as we have opportunity, let us do good to all, especially to those who are of the household of faith.*" This Scripture exhorts us to do good things for everyone, but especially to our family of the believers in Jesus Christ. It begins in our own homes. If a husband comes home from work and takes notice of all the things his wife has done during the day, though he is tired from his own day at work, it will make a big difference in how she feels about it too. She cares for and trains the children, keeps the house, and does the laundry and the cooking, along with all the other ongoing routine tasks she performs. When he acknowledges her diligence, thanks her, and expresses his appreciation for the job she does, it motivates her to keep doing it. Often it is easy to neglect the ones we love the most.

Likewise, when a wife acknowledges her husband's diligence to work to provide for his family and shows some gratitude and praise for what he does, it will energize him and motivate him to know that he too is appreciated and not taken for granted. Our children need encouragement for the things they do and praise for the things they do well. Everyone needs encouragement, and we especially need to make sure we do not neglect the ones in our own house.

We should encourage others and whenever we have the opportunity show appreciation for them, especially other believers. In doing so we can help them to stay more cheerful about what they do. When we acknowledge good deeds and express proper appreciation, to some extent it will help prevent weariness and discouragement from setting in.

When no one else notices what we do, God does notice. He always has and He always will.

Sometimes it takes some time until we see the rewards of doing good, but they will always come, and that is clear in the Word of God. If you care well for your children and do your best to raise them the way God's Word tells you to, you will see the rewards in the way they live. In addition, one day they will come back to thank you. Moreover, God will reward you in eternity, if not even before.

There are many people working behind the scenes. They serve others and do very important things. Some people are more visible and get recognition for what they do because what they are doing is obvious. Often people working behind the scenes make someone else who is more visible look very good but never get any public recognition themselves. God sees, and He always rewards a diligent servant. They will certainly have their rewards in heaven if not here as well. God notices what each member of His Church does. He will make sure each receives his or her appropriate reward, whether it is in this life or in heaven.

Galatians 6:9 says, "*if we do not lose heart,*" and that means do not give up. If we think of the harvest we want, there is the incentive to sow only what will produce that harvest. Moreover, in the appropriate season we will see that harvest.

The way to keep that fresh and alive in our hearts and minds is to wait on God and let Him fill us afresh with renewed courage and hope and vision to keep sowing what we desire to reap. We need to be like eagles that rise up above the storms and see things from a higher perspective. When we wait on God, we begin to see things from His perspective.

Heavenly Father,

I invite Your refreshing river of the Holy Spirit to flow afresh in the hearts of these who are reading this book. May they have insight into what You see in the good they are doing and the diligence with which they do it regularly. Renew their strength, cause them to mount up with wings like eagles, so that they will run and not become weary and they will walk and not faint.

I thank You, Father, for reviving their spirits, their strength, and their joy and for encouraging them to keep doing good, knowing that they will reap a harvest of righteousness in season. In Jesus' name we ask. Amen.

The Dark Times

Blessed is the man Who walks not in the counsel of the ungodly, Nor stands in the path of sinners, Nor sits in the seat of the scornful; But his delight is in the law of the LORD, And in His law he meditates day and night. He shall be like a tree Planted by the rivers of water, That brings forth its fruit in its season, Whose leaf also shall not wither; And whatever he does shall prosper (Psalm 1:1–3).

The spirit of a man is the lamp of the LORD, Searching all the inner depths of his heart (Proverbs 20:27).

And He said to me, "My grace is sufficient for you, for My strength is made perfect in weakness." Therefore most gladly I will rather boast in my infirmities, that the power of Christ may rest upon me (2 Corinthians 12:9).

Sometimes we go through periods of time when things seem very dark or gloomy. We look for the light on our pathway, but even the lamp at our feet seems dim. We put one foot in front of the other and we keep doing what we know to do, but it seems futile. We wonder what we should be doing to make ourselves feel better about ourselves, but it just seems there is no revelation—no light! We seem to be going it alone, seemingly in the dark, while we hope and believe that God is guiding us. In times like these, we may become fearful that we have missed it or maybe God is not directing us at all. We desperately cry out to Him for clarification or confirmation, but it does not seem to be forthcoming.

We do not feel anything, and we do not seem to hear anything either. We ask, we seek, and we knock, and it just seems God does not answer as He said He would. That is exactly what we need to keep doing—just keep doing what we know is right while we walk through this valley of "darkness." We have a new appreciation for the light when in our understanding it turns on after going through a valley of darkness. As we reflect on those dark times, we can see that God was always with us. His hand remained upon us, and His guidance was there even when we could not see anything or feel anything and it seemed we could not hear anything.

These are times when faith carries us when sight cannot direct us. In those times we need to keep waiting on God, reading and meditating on the Word of God, and living according to its instructions and principles, the same as we would if we could understand everything and feel and see and hear what we think we need to during those times.

Sometimes when I go through a valley like this, I feel all alone. It seems there is no one to talk to and no one who can shed any light on my situation. How I long to hear and to have the assurance that I am still in the will of God! If only I knew whether I just need to wait for the light to dawn again, as it does when morning comes and the sun shines again. I wait and expect and pray and learn to trust.

Even though we may feel as though we need to tell people about it when we are called upon to endure a valley, people will not be able to help us. It may be wise to handle it between you and God alone. Sometimes when we do try to talk to people about it, they do not understand, and we end up feeling worse than we did before. These experiences force us back to God alone, and that is what He is waiting for at times like these. God is maturing us into relying totally on Him, and He is bringing us to a place of deep trust and faith in Him. He teaches us by experience that He will never leave us or forsake us. He is the Shepherd of our souls, and come what may, He is with us to the very end.

We are learning to live by the Spirit's voice and God's Word, not our own senses or natural perceptions. When He gives us no new instructions, we just keep doing what we already know to do. Our flesh may feel as though it is going to die, but we are going to be fine if we just wait for God to take us through it. Then, when the joy comes again, we have changed. The truths of God's Word become much more real as you learn by experience to take the hand of the Good Shepherd by faith and let Him take you through these times. He will prove that He can be trusted. Faith is trusting in the invisible.

When you are following the leading of the Holy Spirit during these training times, you will not usually be following the crowd. They probably will not understand you. Let God take you deeper than you ever thought it was possible. When you walk hand in hand with Him while you cannot see anything else, you will become more and more like Him. You will learn the secrets of the kingdom, because you are in communion with the King Himself. Like in a romance, you share the joys and the sorrows. Moreover, the love you have for the One who is holding your hand makes you feel safe even while you feel afraid.

When doubts assail your mind and you challenge your own understanding about what you believe, your faith is growing stronger and God's Word is transforming your mind. He is changing your way of thinking as the Holy Spirit makes the Word alive. Your way of thinking is being changed by the Word Himself, who is the Lord Jesus Christ.

If you are going through the dark night of the soul, let God be your light and your hope and your strength. Remember, Paul said that in our weakness God's strength is made perfect. His power is most effective and most evident in our times of weakness.

When we are in desperate situations and we are powerless to change them ourselves, God is able to speak to us about whatever He wants and do what He sees necessary in us. God has positioned us for that. Our deliverance or victory over the dark times is dependant on Him and our surrender to Him. We begin to understand that in the valleys. That is why these seasons are good for us even though they are not enjoyable. In our dark times, God shines His light into our spirits, and we see what He sees in us and around us. God is light, and when He shines His light into our spirits it shows up anything in us that is contrary to His Word and His will for us.

Sometimes people give us quick fixes, or they at least try to, but in our hearts we know there is a lot more to it and that God is walking us through a valley. There is no quick fix for it. It is not to harm us or to destroy us, but there are no victories without valleys. God wants to bring us out victorious, for His own name's sake. When He accomplishes His will in us and His nature in us reflects Jesus to others on this earth, He is glorified. It points people to Him.

> Heavenly Father,
>
> I pray for those who are going through valleys of sorrow, heartache, broken relationships, or other hardships now. May they know, Lord, that You are carrying them and that their hands are in Yours, even though right now it does not look like it or feel like it and their valley seems too deep to come out of again. Cause Your love to motivate them to finish the race set before them. Strengthen them, and may Your love increase in them so that they will know You intimately. Grant them Your love, mercy, and grace, even in this dark valley that is seemingly hopeless, and cause their

hope to soar again. I ask that You will cause them to rise up like eagles who soar above the clouds and see things from Your perspective. Cause them to overcome, and grant a victorious testimony for each one who is here now. Let them know You more deeply and trust You more completely every day of this journey. Amen.

Preparation

And He Himself gave some to be apostles, some prophets, some evangelists, and some pastors and teachers, for the equipping of the saints for the work of ministry, for the edifying of the body of Christ, till we all come to the unity of the faith and of the knowledge of the Son of God, to a perfect man, to the measure of the stature of the fullness of Christ; that we should no longer be children, tossed to and fro and carried about with every wind of doctrine, by the trickery of men, in the cunning craftiness of deceitful plotting, but, speaking the truth in love, may grow up in all things into Him who is the head—Christ—from whom the whole body, joined and knit together by what every joint supplies, according to the effective working by which every part does its share, causes growth of the body for the edifying of itself in love (Ephesians 4:11–16).

When God calls a person to a specific mission or task, there is a preparation time. Sometimes people in their selfish ambition or fleshly zeal and immaturity set out to accomplish what they think they should instead of waiting for what God actually wants them to do. Sadly, often they are not ready or mature enough, and instead of God opening the way for them, they do it on their own, and the results show it. By the time God is finished with us and He opens the door for us, it may look very different from the way we envisioned it when we first had it in our hearts. Even if it is coming from God, we have to wait for the right timing—God's timing!

Studying Scripture, being able to quote Scripture, and even going to Bible college or seminary do not in themselves equal a calling from God; and they certainly don't automatically authorize people to be in full-time ministry. People need some time to be seasoned. Before they can be in authority, they need to learn how to be under God-ordained authority. There is a difference between being educated and being trained by God.

A call from God is like a dream or consuming desire in us that we very likely did not ever think about before we became Christians. It is something we yearn for, wait for, and intensely desire but cannot do on our own. If we try to produce it on our own, it will not look the way God intended it to look. It will not be nearly as effective as when we are under His authority—hearing the call and following His instructions! God wants to lead us. He is not interested in following us while we devise our own plans. He first wants to teach us how to listen to Him, so that it is God working through us instead of us doing it in our own strength. That is how the Holy Spirit reigns on earth today.

When God calls us to something, we need to listen very carefully to Him as to how He wants to prepare us. He does not want us to bring it about; He wants to do it. He wants us to start being very attentive to Him about the preparation and training He wants to do in our lives. There is a lot more to this than going to an institution to get a degree or diploma or certificate. The true anointing from God does not come from that. It does not come from education. He wants to train people Himself. This happens with God's Word and the Holy Spirit of God working in the hearts of people and renewing minds, bringing about His very nature. He wants His people to be as reflections of His own dear Son so they will shine as lights in the world.

Before people go out to preach the gospel or teach others, they need to be mature enough to be a proper reflection of the Jesus they are preaching about. That makes Jesus Christ much more desirable to those who do not know Him yet. Seasoned saints are effective saints, they are vessels for God's light to shine through, and they are the "salt" of the earth. Light makes darkness manifest, and salt purifies and preserves.

Leaders who are seasoned and mature in godly character are "the fathers and mothers." They are the ones we can look upon as our examples. They are mentors, and they are easy to follow because they themselves are following Christ. They are not doing what they do out of selfish ambition to build their own little kingdom or empire here on earth. They are people who are pointing others to Christ the Anointed One by their own example. When the life backs up what comes out of the mouth, it is very convincing and highly effective. Fathers and mothers of the faith are building God's kingdom.

Those who have paid the price, given themselves to the preparation, and disciplined themselves to live by the Word of God deserve honor, for they truly do what they do because of their love for God. They walk in the Spirit, doing only that which God is showing them to do. Jesus Himself said that if we love Him we will keep His commandments. This is not legalism but obedience out of love for God and love for the truth.

Moses is one example in the Bible of a man who had a great call from God and set out to do it before he quite understood it. When Moses was about forty years old, he went one day to see how his people were doing. He saw how the Egyptians were mistreating and oppressing the Hebrews. He saw an Egyptian beating one of his Hebrew brothers, and he took matters into his own hands. He looked around and, thinking no one was watching, he killed the Egyptian and hid his body in the sand.

The next day he saw two Hebrew men fighting, and he asked one why he was striking his own companion. The man answered Moses by saying, "*Who made you a prince or a judge over us? Are you intending to kill me as you killed the Egyptian?*" (Exodus 2:14). Then Moses realized that people knew he had killed an Egyptian. Pharaoh found out about it and was very angry with Moses, so Moses had to run for his life. He went to the land of Midian and was there for about another forty years before he had a visitation from God in the desert, where he was tending his father-in-law, Jethro's, flock.

The Angel of the Lord appeared to Moses in the flame of a fire in the midst of a bush. The bush was on fire but not consumed. Moses saw this strange sight and went for a closer look. He heard God calling him by name from the bush, saying, "*Moses! Moses!*" He answered, "*Here I am.*" Then God asked Moses to take off his shoes, for the ground was holy because of God's presence. During this visitation, God told Moses that He was responding to the cries of the Hebrews who were in bondage in Egypt and were oppressed and treated very badly by the Egyptians. God then explained to Moses that He wanted to send him to deliver the people from the slavery (Exodus 3).

Finally, the time is ripe for Moses, and God sends him to Egypt as God's deliverer for His people. After a series of plagues, which God brought upon the Egyptians to show His power, Pharaoh finally let them go. Moses then led them through the Red Sea on dry ground, while all the Egyptians who followed them drowned (Exodus 3–15). After they crossed the Red Sea and they were safe on the other side, they sang a beautiful song of praise to God for the victory He brought (Exodus 15:1–21). All the glory goes to God, for it was clearly His doing.

There must have been some humbling, deep work of God's Spirit going on in Moses' life during his forty years of serving as a shepherd in the desert in Midian. Moses was fully prepared and trained by God, even though he had personal fears and struggles about what God was asking of him. When God visited him again and gave him instructions for the mission in Egypt, the time was right. He endured a lot, including the complaining of the people he had to lead, but God brought the victory. The mission for which God prepared him was now taking place. It was by the hand of God. Even though many of the people died in the wilderness, it was their own doing, not the plan of God. God called Moses to lead them out, and he did. God said He would always be "with Moses," and very obviously, He was.

If we wait for God, He will be with us too. If we know Jesus personally, the Holy Spirit is living in us, but in ministry or service to God we must wait for Him to lead us so that He will be with us in that same manner as well. As I said earlier, He does not follow our plans and back those up with His power, but He backs up what He says. That is why we need to listen first and when we hear, then obey.

Here is the prayer Jesus gave to His disciples. Let us pray it now:

Our Father in heaven, Hallowed be Your name. Your kingdom come. Your will be done On earth as it is in heaven. Give us this day our daily bread. And forgive us our debts, As we forgive our debtors. And do not lead us into temptation, But deliver us from the evil one. For Yours is the kingdom and the power and the glory forever. Amen (Matthew 6:9–13).

Freedom

Now the Lord is the Spirit; and where the Spirit of the Lord is, there is liberty (2 Corinthians 3:17).

Jesus said,

"The Spirit of the LORD is upon Me, Because He has anointed Me To preach the gospel to the poor; He has sent Me to heal the brokenhearted, To proclaim liberty to the captives And recovery of sight to the blind, To set at liberty those who are oppressed; To proclaim the acceptable year of the LORD" (Luke 4:18–19).

"If you abide in My word, you are My disciples indeed. And you shall know the truth, and the truth shall make you free." They answered Him, "We are Abraham's descendants, and have never been in bondage to anyone. How can You say, 'You will be made free?'" Jesus answered them, "Most assuredly, I say to you, whoever commits sin is a slave of sin. And a slave does not abide in the house forever, but a son abides forever. Therefore if the Son makes you free, you shall be free indeed" (John 8:31–36).

When we come to Christ, we become a brand new creation. The new birth happens supernaturally. It is as though we "conceived" the Holy Spirit and a new person begins to develop on the inside of us. He transforms us, making us in nature like Himself. As this new person or new nature of Christ begins to grow in us, it gradually replaces the old carnal or sinful nature, which we were born with when our physical birth took place. When we invite Jesus to come and take over our lives, He comes to dwell in us by His Holy Spirit. Now we are spiritually alive, connected to God the Father through Jesus the Son, who sent the same Spirit who raised Him from the dead to come and live in us.

Before we knew Christ Jesus, we were in bondage, slaves to that old sinful nature. When He came and made us alive in Him, He gave us freedom to become the children of God. He made us free to serve Him and not to live by the rules and regulations of religious bondage.

In John 13:34, 35 Jesus says, "A new commandment I give to you, that you love one another; as I have loved you, that you also love one another. By this all will know that you are My disciples, if you have love for one another." If we love the way He loves we do not need to be weighed down with minute thoughts about what is right and wrong. We do not need to focus on the things we should and should not do in order to please God. When we focus our eyes on Jesus and our purpose to love others it is not a heavy yoke to bear. It is not burdensome. The law showed us what sin is, it did not have the power or the "grace" to break its hold on our lives. The Cross and the resurrection of Jesus did that. If we love as Jesus said we should, we will not break His commandments. They are all included in the love walk. He made it simple.

Then when Christ makes us free, we are to walk in the new freedom that He has given us. That does not mean each one just does whatever seems right for him or her. It means we are free to obey God and do what His Holy Spirit leads us to do. It is freedom from the domination or control of other people and religious bondages, but not freedom to do whatever we want to do. It is freedom to obey God and His Word.

It means there is freedom to hear from God and give expression to what He is saying to us and what He is asking us to do. To behave in ways that are consistent with Him, His Holy nature, His will, and His Word is a blessed and joyous liberty that the Holy Spirit produces in believers.

All believers have access to God. Everyone has the privilege and freedom to hear His voice. Among a group of believers where they give the Spirit of the Lord His rightful place of leadership, each one will have freedom to hear and to grow, without pressure to conform externally to another. Then we can celebrate our uniqueness and not feel external restraints. The Holy Spirit frees us to be the person God meant us to become. Then the expression of who we are in Christ and how God made each one of us becomes apparent and significant. Who we are determines what we will do in the body of Christ. It does not work the other way around! The Spirit of the Lord brings that liberty to the individual and to the Church—especially where everyone allows Him to do so.

Leaders need to recognize this and encourage it. When leaders are insecure and want people to look only to them for God's direction, it does not help believers to look to God for their own direction. This hinders the liberty believers should be experiencing in the Church. A leader who surrenders him or herself to the leading of the Holy Spirit and operates under His authority will not dominate or try to control the people. Where the Spirit of the Lord has free reign, there will not be any hidden agendas. When leaders want to control what people will do, they are trying to replace what the Holy Spirit wants to do for people. This has kept many people from reaching their potential in the body of Christ. It has discouraged and wounded many who have been under the hand of these leaders. They do not have the best interests of the people at heart, but they desire power; human ambition drives them. They have hidden agendas, insecurities, and a desire to control or manipulate others.

God wants shepherds after his own heart to lead and feed his people. Where there is freedom in the Holy Spirit the joy of the Lord abounds as well. In addition, the joy of the Lord is our strength. When our joy is gone, so is our strength. Joy is a great motivator. It keeps us alive and energized so that we want to keep serving the Lord with all our hearts.

I perceive that many who are reading this have been confused and wounded by being in churches where they feared the leaders instead of being able to respect them. They were afraid to speak from their hearts or ask the questions they really wanted to ask, because they feared rejection. Many have drawn back from participating with their gifts, talents, and abilities because in the past it brought great hurt and discouragement into their lives. Others questioned if God was there for them, even heard their prayers, or if He saw or cared about what was happening to them.

God wants you to take heart and seek Him again with your whole heart. Seek Him as your best friend. He can be trusted. Many have seen God through the picture of their experiences in the Church, and they cannot accept that He is a good God, a loving God, and a good provider, because they have been so disillusioned by their personal experiences in the church, many of them at the hands of controlling leaders. Where is the love I heard about when I first came to the church, and what about all the hypocrisy, and what about all the wounded who are cast aside as though the wounds were never inflicted?

You need to reconcile these questions between you and God. Draw close to Him, and He will draw close to you. He will heal you of your wounds, and He will restore your wounded spirit and your wounded soul as you invite Him to do so. As you begin to heal, ask Him to help you release and let go of the things that happened to you by forgiving those who caused them. Then the torment will leave your mind and you will experience the joy of the liberty of the Holy Spirit in your life again.

Though God speaks to all of us and leads us by His Spirit, He sets leaders into the church offices to watch over the flock. They are there to lead, preach, teach and give direction to the church. They protect us from error and keep us in the truth by preaching the Word of God to us regularly.

There are many wonderful pastors laboring in the work of the Lord and caring for the flock of God all over the earth. We need to love and respect them and honor them for who they are in Christ. We must not forget their labor of love to us as members of Christ's church. Hebrews 13:17 says, "Obey those who rule over you, and be submissive, for they watch out for your souls, as those who must give account. Let them do so with joy and not with grief, for that would be unprofitable for you."

Grief

A merry heart makes a cheerful countenance, But by sorrow of the heart the spirit is broken (Proverbs 15:13).

Hope deferred makes the heart sick, But when the desire comes, it is a tree of life (Proverbs 13:12).

Surely He has borne our griefs And carried our sorrows; Yet we esteemed Him stricken, Smitten by God, and afflicted. But He was wounded for our transgressions, He was bruised for our iniquities; The chastisement for our peace was upon Him, And by His stripes we are healed (Isaiah 53:4–5).

In this world, we face our share of sorrows and grief as well as joy and gladness. The grief we experience when a loved one passes away is one of the deepest sorrows in our lives. Though people around us are kind and look for words and ways to comfort us, though it all helps us through the valley of grief, it seems nothing can take away the agony of that grief. First, there is the shock of the accidental death or the diagnosis of a terminal illness that without a miracle from God will separate that loved one from us. These are very difficult days or years in life when only God can comfort us and heal us of our pain. These are lonely times, times of doubting God's goodness, and times of anger, depression, and maybe even bitterness. Throughout the stages of grief we go through, God is with us, even when it does not feel like it. Sometimes it seems as though He is far away. It feels as though the pain is so great that we cannot even experience God's presence. But He *is* present with us, and He is taking us on the healing journey, even though we may at times doubt that because it hurts so much to be suffering such an incredible loss.

It may takes months or even years, but slowly we adapt to living with our loss, without that loved one here to talk to and have fellowship with and share our lives with. We will always miss them, but we heal, move on, and gradually start to build a life without them. These are major adjustments, and God understands that.

The death of a loved one, no doubt one of the greatest sorrows, is not the only loss we will grieve in this life. Going through a divorce is a very devastating experience for many people too. Regardless of who was at fault, the loss is huge. If there are children involved, especially young children, they do not have the ability to process the breakup of the family and understand it. Often they think they are somehow to blame and they live with guilt because of it. In many divorces, they are the ones who suffer the most. Often they are too young to understand or know what they are feeling. They cannot describe or process that in a way that brings healing. They cannot express it or even understand that it is not their fault in any way. They may internalize the pain and anger, resulting in depression. They cannot grieve and recover in a healthy manner, because they cannot identify the root problem. It is often suppressed and later on expressed in ways that are misunderstood.

Sometimes people have had great goals, and when they come to the realization that they cannot achieve them, they mourn the loss of their dreams. The losses may be invisible, but they are nonetheless very real, as is the grief they cause. It may be a job loss or a relationship with a close friend that has suddenly gone wrong. It is therapeutic to recognize these losses and give ourselves permission to grieve over them in a healthy way. If the pain turns inward, it becomes suppressed grief.

Sometimes loss comes in the form of huge disappointments when our expectations are not met. When we have expectations that seemed just and right to us but something happens to prevent them being fulfilled, our hearts are shattered. We sometimes shrug it off and do not even fully acknowledge it to ourselves. Unexpressed pain goes deep into our hearts, and there it lies, buried. We need to resurrect it in order to find release and healing so it will not trigger negative responses from us anymore. They were symptoms of the suppressed grief. If we have not been able to express our emotions in a healthy way, they will come out sideways, but they will come out somehow. If we have not channeled our emotions in a healthy way, they may be misdirected. Then we take things out on someone or something other than what we are really upset, hurting, or angry about.

When our health is not what it once was and we long to be strong again, well again, and able to do the things again that we once enjoyed without giving it a second thought, there is a grieving process going on in our lives. We have lost the ability to do the things that brought us satisfaction, laughter, and fun. It is the loss of what once was and what we enjoyed. It is normal and fine to acknowledge it and to talk about it to someone else and then receive comfort from God Himself. Sometimes talking about it helps us to put it into proper perspective. Someone else with an objective viewpoint or encouraging words of empathy can make a big difference during times such as these.

Suppressed grief can have very negative effects on us without us realizing what is happening to us. Sometimes things happen that we need to allow ourselves to grieve over openly, but we do not do that, because we do not feel free to talk about it, we believe no one else cares about it, and we think we just need to keep quiet and get over it. Sometimes we need to let it surface and talk to someone who will listen with compassion and understand what is happening to us. It is perfectly fine to find some help through counseling or from a good mentor or Christian friend.

If a merry heart does us good like a medicine, then it makes sense that a sad heart or broken spirit will do the opposite.

Joy

When the LORD brought back the captivity of Zion, We were like those who dream. Then our mouth was filled with laughter, And our tongue with singing. Then they said among the nations, "The LORD has done great things for them." The LORD has done great things for us, And we are glad. Bring back our captivity, O LORD, As the streams in the South. Those who sow in tears Shall reap in joy. He who continually goes forth weeping, Bearing seed for sowing, Shall doubtless come again with rejoicing, Bringing his sheaves with him (Psalm 126:1–6).

This is a psalm, or song, about the people of God returning to their homeland when God overturned their captivity. They were in captivity in Babylon for seventy years when suddenly it turned around and their deliverance came. Though Cyrus proclaimed liberty to God's people who were in captivity in Babylon, God Himself brought it about. He spoke to them many years before this all happened; it was His doing. God did not allow the captivity so that His people could be destroyed but for them to be refined as gold.

Though God had His hand on them the whole time and to Him it was divine planning for their future, to the captives the deliverance came so suddenly that it seemed like a dream. It seemed too good to be true. Their years of weeping and hopelessness, depression, and despondency turned into overwhelming joy. They laughed, and they sang songs of deliverance. While they were in captivity they did not play their harps, but now their songs and dances returned. The nations, or the heathen neighbors, spoke of it as news. They referred to it as Jehovah, the God of Israel, doing great things for His people. They recognized that the God of Israel had power their gods did not have. However, God's own people spoke of God as their Sovereign Lord who freed them from captivity, and they could not contain their joy, since their sorrow had been so great for so long. It was as though they had waited for many years for something that it seemed would never happen. They sowed in tears, and that likely included tears of sorrow for their hardships, remorse for sin, and regret for disobedience to their God, which brought about their captivity, and tears of repentance for all of it. Then one day their sowing in tears turned into a harvest of joy. They now had the liberty of returning to their homeland.

When they returned to Zion, they still had some burdens to overcome, and there were still many of them left behind in Babylon. They probably still sowed some tears of tender intercession for those left behind who needed to act with courage and take hold of the liberty they now had to return home. When tears of intercession flow from a tender heart toward God and there is godly sorrow for sin, a harvest of joy and rejoicing will surely follow when the season is right.

David, though he suffered the consequences of his own sin, repented genuinely before God and asked the Lord to restore to him the joy of His salvation that the sin and sorrow of it had taken away from him. Psalm 51 is a record of how completely and openly David repented of his sin of murder and adultery. In verse 12 he said, "*Restore to me the joy of Your salvation, And uphold me by Your generous Spirit.*" In verse 14 he said, "*Deliver me from the guilt of bloodshed, O God, The God of my salvation, And my tongue shall sing aloud of Your righteousness."* In verse 15 he added, *"O Lord, open my lips, And my mouth shall show forth Your praise."*

Joseph suffered greatly for the sins of others who hated him. His own brothers sold him into slavery in Egypt and then lied to their father about what happened to him. Potiphar's wife lied, saying that Joseph tried to rape her, and then he was sent to prison for something he did not do. Rather, he refused her advances and ran from her because he was not going to sin against his God or anyone else. He suffered greatly, but he purposed in his heart to live righteously regardless of the injustices done against him. One day, overnight, his captivity turned as well. They brought him into the palace, and he became the prime minister of Egypt. He was second-in-command only to Pharaoh. No doubt there were tears of sorrow and tender tears of intercession as he sought the Lord for his deliverance when he was falsely accused and was serving a sentence in prison. However, there came a season when he reaped a great harvest of joy that must have exceeded anything he ever dreamed possible. God brought it about. The dreams Joseph had when he was a young teenager now came to fruition. Great sorrow turned into great joy and rejoicing.

Job went through devastating times when he lost his children, his possessions, and his health. It must have been very grievous and hard to understand how God could let him suffer so greatly and go through the grief of losing even his own family. The time came when his sorrow turned into joy and God gave him greater possessions than he had before, and he had another seven sons and three daughters. Job 42:12 tells us that *"the LORD blessed the latter days of Job more than his beginning."* At the end of the book of Job, it says he lived 140 years after all of that happened, and he lived to see his children and grandchildren for four generations. Though he went through desperate times and suffered greatly, he too reaped a harvest of joy in the end.

Though the reasons for the hardships and sorrow we go through are often very different, if we sow our tears with tenderness of heart toward God, we too will reap a harvest of joy, and there will come a time of rejoicing for us.

Regardless of the cause of our tears, if we sow them as "liquid prayers" unto God, He will heal us and restore us. When that season is over, we too will have songs of joy and thanksgiving and praise to God for turning our sorrows into joy.

Our Father who is in Heaven,

We ask for the courage to go through the valley of tears with the help of Your Holy Spirit, who strengthens and comforts us. Help us, and remind us to keep our focus, our minds, stayed on you so that we can experience Your peace in the midst of our grief and our sorrow. Take our hands and keep us strong in the power of Your might so that we will not falter or faint but courageously cross the valleys of sorrow and tears. Teach us to rest in You and lean on You so that You carry us until we are completely whole again. Lead us into victory so we can rejoice in the harvest of righteousness that godly sorrow brings. Thank You for turning our sorrow into joy because we put our trust in You. In Jesus' name. Amen.

Peace

You will keep him in perfect peace, Whose mind is stayed on You, Because he trusts in You (Isaiah 26:3).

Be anxious for nothing, but in everything by prayer and supplication, with thanksgiving, let your requests be made known to God; and the peace of God, which surpasses all understanding, will guard your hearts and minds through Christ Jesus. Finally, brethren, whatever things are true, whatever things are noble, whatever things are just, whatever things are pure, whatever things are lovely, whatever things are of good report, if there is any virtue and if there is anything praiseworthy—meditate on these things. The things which you learned and received and heard and saw in me, these do, and the God of peace will be with you (Philippians 4:6–9).

The word *mind* in Isaiah 26:3 also means our "creative imagination."[2] That would include our meditation. The things we think about deeply and continually will affect our behavior and our emotions. It may take an act of our will at times to think about the good things in our lives, but if we do that, we will feel better emotionally and mentally. If we allow our minds to dwell on the things in our lives that cause us stress and result in fretting, worrying, and

---

[2] *The New Spirit Filled Life Bible* (Thomas Nelson, 2002), 901.

being anxious, it will affect us negatively. It is therapeutic for us spiritually, mentally, emotionally, and even physically to dwell on the good things of God. He gives us the comforts, assurances, and promises in His Word that are like medicine for our general wellbeing. When our minds are at peace, we feel better overall. Continuous turmoil and mental stress will eventually affect our physical health as well.

Taking control of our minds and our thoughts is not an easy thing for most people. It takes active discipline and constant vigilance on our part to apply the truths of the Word of God to our thought life. As we do that, we learn more and more how to control what we think about, and especially how to watch the things we allow our minds to dwell on. What we put into our minds the most will affect us the most. If we regularly put the Word of God into our hearts and minds, it is going to affect us very positively. That is how our minds are renewed. The Bible itself clearly tells us that in Romans 12:1–2:

> *I beseech you therefore, brethren, by the mercies of God, that you present your bodies a living sacrifice, holy, acceptable to God, which is your reasonable service. And do not be conformed to this world, but be transformed by the renewing of your mind, that you may prove what is that good and acceptable and perfect will of God.*

The initial peace we experience from God is when we enter into a relationship with Jesus. Through the shed blood of Christ and His death, we are reconciled to God and we enter into peace with God. Romans 5:1–2 says, *"Therefore, having been justified by faith, we have peace with God through our Lord Jesus Christ, through whom also we have access by faith into this grace in which we stand, and rejoice in hope of the glory of God."* Verse 10 says, *"For if when we were enemies we were reconciled to God through the* death of His Son, much more, having been reconciled, we shall be saved by His life."

When we know Jesus Christ as our personal Lord and Savior, His peace abides in us. This peace is evident when in the natural there is absolutely no reason for us to have peace. When adversity comes and bad news or a negative report comes to us about someone we love or ourselves and this peace manifests, it is the peace of God. We could not have this peace without Him, and certainly our circumstances would not produce it or even permit it at such times. It is supernatural peace from the Holy Spirit.

In John 14:27 Jesus said, *"Peace I leave with you, My peace I give to you; not as the world gives do I give to you. Let not your heart be troubled, neither let it be afraid."* And then again in John 16:32–33 He said,

> *"Indeed the hour is coming, yes, has now come, that you will be scattered, each to his own, and will leave Me alone. And yet I am not alone, because the Father is with Me. These things I have spoken to you, that in Me you may have peace. In the world you will have tribulation; but be of good cheer, I have overcome the world."*

When we do the will of God and we are peacemakers, we experience peace ourselves. We experience peace when we do our best to live peaceably with our own husbands, children, and families. This peace will flow out to our brothers and sisters in Christ and to our neighbors in the world around us.

Romans 12:18 says, *"If it is possible, as much as depends on you, live peaceably with all men."* In Matthew 5:9 Jesus said, *"Blessed are the peacemakers, For they shall be called sons of God."* It is not always possible for us to live at peace with everyone. What is important though, is that it is in our hearts to make peace and to live at peace with others whenever we have any control over the situation. If someone else refuses to be at peace with us, we cannot control that, but we need to have the heart attitude of peacemakers.

This wonderful exhortation from the Scriptures will help us to live in peace and experience the peace of God if we apply it to our own lives:

> *Therefore, as the elect of God, holy and beloved, put on tender mercies, kindness, humility, meekness, longsuffering; bearing with one another, and forgiving one another, if anyone has a complaint against another; even as Christ forgave you, so you also must do. But above all these things put on love, which is the bond of perfection. And let the peace of God rule in your hearts, to which also you were called in one body; and be thankful. Let the word of Christ dwell in you richly in all wisdom, teaching and admonishing one another in psalms and hymns and spiritual songs, singing with grace in your hearts to the Lord* (Colossians 3:12–16).

"Great peace have those who love Your law, And nothing causes them to stumble" (Psalm 119:165). My prayer for you today is the blessing from Numbers 6:24–26. The Lord told Moses to instruct Aaron and his sons to bless the children of Israel by saying this to them: *"The LORD bless you and keep you; The LORD make His face shine upon you, And be gracious to you; The LORD lift up His countenance upon you, And give you peace."*

Health

Do not be wise in your own eyes; Fear the LORD and depart from evil. It will be health to your flesh, And strength to your bones (Proverbs 3:7–8).

My son, give attention to my words; Incline your ear to my sayings. Do not let them depart from your eyes; Keep them in the midst of your heart; For they are life to those who find them, And health to all their flesh (Proverbs 4:20–22).

He who speaks truth declares righteousness, But a false witness, deceit. There is one who speaks like the piercings of a sword, But the tongue of the wise promotes health (Proverbs 12:17–18).

Beloved, I pray that you may prosper in all things and be in health, just as your soul prospers. For I rejoiced greatly when brethren came and testified of the truth that is in you, just as you walk in the truth. I have no greater joy than to hear that my children walk in truth (3 John 1:2–4).

When we think about health, we think about freedom from pain, physical strength, a nice, healthy countenance—an obvious picture of physical well-being. When people feel good physically, their eyes are full of life and often tend to sparkle. When they are sick, the sparkle is gone. Pain is sometimes evident in a person's eyes.

Depression often accompanies a lengthy illness or a diagnosis of a terminal illness. Though this writing is not about healing per se, it is about health, which is general well-being in all areas of our lives. We cannot prevent everything that happens to us. Some things we have no control over at all. Sometimes that includes our physical health. Often people have to lose their health before they truly appreciate it. Only then does it become obvious to some people how important good health is and how much it has to do with our quality of life on this earth.

Unless the Lord comes first for some, all people on earth are all going to die a physical death. Many of us do not like to even think about it, but it is a fact of life that this physical body, the vessel of clay, will one day die, because it is not immortal. Some day God will resurrect us with immortal bodies, but the ones we live in now are subject to decay.

Sometimes babies are born with health problems. Certain people are more susceptible to some diseases due to genetic factors. However, the Word of God tells us that we can do some things to prevent as much of it as possible by following the instructions God has given us in His Word.

When we think of health, we think mostly of the physical body, but a picture of health according to the Word of God goes deeper than what shows up in our physical bodies in the form of pain or physical discomfort or inconvenience. Some of the Scriptures quoted are referring to deliverance from false doctrines and behavior that hinders our general well-being. We are told not to be wise in our own eyes or in our own opinions. It says to *"Fear the LORD and depart from evil."* We must turn away from things that are useless and do not promote health or well-being in our own lives or in the lives of those around us.

Proverbs 8:13 says to fear the LORD is to hate evil: pride, arrogance, and perverse speech, the things God hates. That means we should have the same heart attitude toward things that are contrary to the Word of God as God Himself has. We must come into agreement with God and His Word and purpose in our hearts to do all God has given us the grace to do in order to live according to it. This will be health to our flesh (our bodies) and strength or drink to our bones. Brittle bones are not healthy bones. Fear of God and departing from anything contrary to God's Word will be like drink or "*strength*" to our bones. That is promoting good health.

"*The tongue of the wise promotes health.*" Our tongues can be instruments of God that declare righteousness when we speak His truth. His truth is all that is according to His Word. When we do that, we are using our tongues wisely and we promote health. Speaking truth and declaring righteousness protects our own well-being as well as that of those around us. These things do us good like medicine, are prevention and deliverance, and bring about wholeness and restoration of God's order to all areas of our lives.

John wrote in 3 John that he had no greater joy than to hear that his spiritual children are walking in truth, and that is what he was hearing from others about them. He wanted them to prosper in all things and be in health just as their souls prospered. When they were walking in truth, rightly applying God's Word to their lives, it would go well with them in every area of their lives. "*All things*" includes their mental, emotional, and physical well-being. "*Prosper in all things*" includes their material needs as well. Blessed were they if they feared the Lord, spoke truth, and walked in love as God's Word instructed them. The same is true for us if we pay close attention to the Word of God.

The few preceding verses instruct us to:

Not be wise in our own eyes or opinions
Fear the Lord and depart from evil
Pay attention to the Word of God

Incline our ears to hear God's Word
Do not let the words of God depart from our eyes
Keep them in the midst of our hearts
Speak truth and declare righteousness
Promote health with our tongues

When we do those things, we are being peacemakers and we are promoting the love and unity of the Holy Spirit according to God's Word. Peace in our hearts is much more conducive to good health. God's Word says it is health to our flesh. However, it is God's Word applied that makes the difference in our lives—not just quoting it like a mantra or something. The truth sets us free when we apply the truth that we know to our own lives. It does not set us free until we let it get on the inside of us.

In John 8:32 Jesus said, *"And you shall know the truth, and the truth shall make you free."* However, if we isolate that verse and do not read the previous one, we are taking it out of context. We must include what Jesus said in the previous verse, John 8:31: *"If you abide in My word, you are My disciples indeed."*

He is telling those who believe that if they abide in His Word they are His disciples. In addition, when they are His disciples and they have come into agreement with what He is teaching them, then their knowledge of the truth will set them free. Truth we do not apply to our lives will not set us free. We have to get it into our hearts.

We can do some very practical things to prevent health problems too. We need to eat right and exercise. We need to learn to manage stress, get enough sleep and rest, and all those practical things. Many people have written books about health, prevention, eating right, and exercising, and some of course are very helpful for us. However, the greatest of all is the one that God inspired, and that is His Word.

"All Scripture is given by inspiration of God, and is profitable for doctrine, for reproof, for correction, for instruction in righteousness, that the man of God may be complete, thoroughly equipped for every good work" (2 Timothy 3:16–17). God inspired the written Word. To all who will heed its instructions and wisdom, it is the manual for life. It will be health to every part of our being if we give it an important place in our lives. Our lives will certainly go better with the Word of God as our manual for life than if we do not apply it to our daily lives. It is a promise of eternal life when we die, but it is also wisdom and instruction for a purposeful and successful life here on this earth for those who love and serve God with all their hearts. It is full of promises for all those who love God's Word and give it an important place in their lives!

We are three-part beings—spirit, soul, and body. Our spirits get information from God. Our souls decide what we will do with that information. With our bodies we live out the decisions that our souls have made. If our souls are not doing what the spirit is hearing from the Holy Spirit, our souls will be miserable, and it will show up in our physical bodies in some way. There is a conflict there, and we are not at peace or happy, because we are disobeying God. They all work together to make the whole person.

God is in the process of restoring what He always intended for us, and we have to agree with Him and abide by His Word to experience the blessings of what He has made available to us. They come to us on His conditions, and that is something we sometimes forget. We cannot claim His promises without recognizing and meeting the conditions He has given us.

Guilt

Now we know that whatever the law says, it says to those who are under the law, that every mouth may be stopped, and all the world may become guilty before God. Therefore by the deeds of the law no flesh will be justified in His sight, for by the law is the knowledge of sin. But now the righteousness of God apart from the law is revealed, being witnessed by the Law and the Prophets, even the righteousness of God, through faith in Jesus Christ, to all and on all who believe. For there is no difference; for all have sinned and fall short of the glory of God, being justified freely by His grace through the redemption that is in Christ Jesus, whom God set forth as a propitiation by His blood, through faith, to demonstrate His righteousness, because in His forbearance God had passed over the sins that were previously committed, to demonstrate at the present time His righteousness, that He might be just and the justifier of the one who has faith in Jesus (Romans 3:19–26).

Then they said to one another, "We are truly guilty concerning our brother, for we saw the anguish of his soul when he pleaded with us, and we would not hear; therefore this distress has come upon us." And Reuben answered them, saying, "Did I not speak to you, saying, 'Do not sin against the boy'; and you would not listen? Therefore behold, his blood is now required of us." But they did not know that Joseph understood them, for he spoke to them through an interpreter. And he turned himself away from them and wept. Then he returned to them again, and talked with them. And he took Simeon from them and bound him before their eyes (Genesis 42:21–24).

When Joseph's brothers saw that their father was dead, they said, "Perhaps Joseph will hate us, and may actually repay us for all the evil which we did to him." So they sent messengers to Joseph, saying, "Before your father died he commanded, saying, 'Thus you shall say to Joseph: "I beg you, please forgive the trespass of your brothers and their sin; for they did evil to you."' Now, please, forgive the trespass of the servants of the God of your father." And Joseph wept when they spoke to him. Then his brothers also went and fell down before his face, and they said, "Behold, we are your servants." Joseph said to them, "Do not be afraid, for am I in the place of God? But as for you, you meant evil against me; but God meant it for good, in order to bring it about as it is this day, to save many people alive. Now therefore, do not be afraid; I will provide for you and your little ones." And he comforted them and spoke kindly to them (Genesis 50:15–21).

Be sober, be vigilant; because your adversary the devil walks about like a roaring lion, seeking whom he may devour (1 Peter 5:8).

The right kind of guilt brings conviction, which leads to turning away from sin or wrongdoing. The law showed us that we are sinners but could not justify us from our sin. The death of Jesus and His shed blood did that, and it becomes our personal experience when we believe that in our hearts and confess that with our mouths. Then we receive justification from our sins, and we are no longer guilty. Ephesians 2:8–9 says, *"For by grace you have been saved through faith, and that not of yourselves; it is the gift of God, not of works, lest anyone should boast."* That is a true and a good guilt to experience or become conscious of, because that conviction causes us to turn to Christ and receive Him as Savior and Lord.

That kind of guilt brings about eternal life. It is appropriate and does not leave us without hope but points us to Jesus as the one who sets us free from our guilt of sin. Jesus, shortly before His death and resurrection, told His disciples that when He left this earth, He would send them another Comforter and Helper. In John 16:8–11 He said, *"And when He has come, He will convict the world of sin, and of righteousness, and of judgment: of sin, because they do not believe in Me; of righteousness, because I go to My Father and you see Me no more; of judgment, because the ruler of this world is judged."*

The Holy Spirit convicts people to make them conscious of their sin and their need of salvation and then opens their understanding to how they can receive that. Along with the conviction of sin, the Holy Spirit opens their understanding to the fact that righteousness is available and that ultimate judgment will come to those who reject this salvation.

The guilt that conviction brings is for the benefit of those who experience it so they can come to repentance and be free of it through Christ's provision for all who make the choice. Everyone in the world is guilty in this sense. Christ, only, can take this guilt away.

There is another kind of guilt and that is for things we do that are not righteous. It is guilt that is directly dependant on things we have done individually. An example of this is what Joseph's brothers did to him. They knew very well that what they were doing was sinful. They did it anyway, because they were jealous and envious of him and they were going to get rid of him. They sold him to the Ishmaelites, who took him to Egypt. Then they lied to their father by telling him they did not know what happened to him. Furthermore, they put an animal's blood on his special garment that their father had given to him and took it to their father. That led their father to believe a wild animal had killed Joseph. He mourned greatly over his son's death for a long time.

Then many years later, there was a severe famine in the land. The only food was in Egypt, because of the plan that God gave Joseph to store up in advance for the years of famine. The brothers had to go to Egypt for food, and they had no idea that they would meet the brother whom they betrayed many years before. In Genesis 42, we read the story of how they were at Joseph's mercy and God brought them face to face with what they had done all those years ago.

Joseph made them squirm a bit when he put them in prison for three days and then told them that one of them had to stay when the others took the provisions back home. He kept Simeon and told the others that in order to get anything in the future and see Simeon again they had to bring Benjamin back to Egypt with them. The brothers knew how much grief this would cause their father, Jacob. Joseph had no plan to harm any of them. Although he recognized all of them, they had no idea that they were dealing with their own brother who was now ruling over them, as revealed in the dreams he had many years before.

After Jacob died, the brothers feared that Joseph would take revenge. Therefore, they sent messengers to Joseph, telling him that before their father died he had requested that Joseph forgive his brothers for the terrible things they had done to him. There is no record in the Scriptures of Jacob having said this. Perhaps the brothers devised another lie to protect themselves. They must have been very afraid of what Joseph would do to them after their father was gone. They were guilty of doing terrible things, and even though Joseph acknowledged that their evil intentions helped to fulfill God's plan for his life and he had no plans to repay their evil deeds, they still had the guilt and the fear that accompanied it. These are consequences of actual guilt.

There is also false guilt. Sometimes we feel guilty over things we had no control over and still have no control over. We feel guilty over things we cannot change. Maybe we let someone else down because we could not live up to his or her expectations, and we carry the guilt. This leads to feelings of condemnation. This is very destructive, and there is no answer to this kind of guilt. The only solution is to get rid of it, because it does not belong to us.

False guilt is very common, and we overcome it by facing it directly and acknowledging it for what it really is. We "feel" guilty about something. Guilty feelings that have no justification are just that: "feelings" of guilt. The Word of God, the name of Jesus, the blood of Jesus, and the Holy Spirit are the weapons we have against false guilt. We can evaluate what we are feeling or experiencing according to the Word of God, asking the Holy Spirit to show us the truth about it. If we experience irrational guilt and there is no scriptural reason for why we feel guilty, then we have to resist it by praying and speaking the Word of God, which is truth, to get rid of those feelings and any condemnation.

I believe many people struggle with false guilt. The enemy uses it to condemn them, make them feel unworthy so that they will think God cannot use them for His purposes. He works hard to make them feel that they cannot live a victorious Christian life because of things that have happened, even if they had no control over them and could not have prevented them. God wants us to live a life of victory and not a life of defeat, so we have to learn to wield the sword of the Spirit, which is the Word of God (Ephesians 6:17). It becomes a sword when we have it on the inside of us and we are living in line with it. This is righteous armor. We have it in our hearts, we speak it with our mouths, and then victory comes.

First Peter 5:8–9 says the devil acts like a roaring lion and his intent is to devour us. He likes to attack us when we are weak and find cowardly strategies to discourage and defeat us and ultimately destroy us. He likes to remind us of all that is wrong with us and why the Lord would not want to use us, and on and on it goes. We have to resist him aggressively, and we do that with the Word, the name and blood of Jesus, and the Holy Spirit's help in praying and discerning what is going on in the spirit realm.

Our adversary likes to set traps for us, pressure us through negative circumstances, and then finally get us to bow to what he wants for us. We have to know the truth and use the sword of the Spirit to defeat the adversary, who is the devil himself. First John 4:4 says, *"You are of God, little children, and have overcome them, because He who is in you is greater than he who is in the world."* False guilt is a lie, and we have to get rid of lies by replacing them with truth.

So pick up the sword, wield it, rise up, and live victoriously in Christ, because that is His plan for you. Speak the Word of God and put down the lies of the enemy by defeating his accusations and lies with God's Word. *"Yet in all these things we are more than conquerors through Him who loved us"* (Romans 8:37).

Heavenly Father,

I thank you that we are more than conquerors through Jesus Christ, who loves us with an everlasting love. Thank You for the promise that absolutely nothing—no devil, no circumstances, and no trials or hardships—can separate us from Your love. If You, the Living and the One True God, are for us, then who can be against us? There is no one like You, for You alone are the Almighty One. Amen.

How to Be Used by God Without Being Used by People

Therefore, as the elect of God, holy and beloved, put on tender mercies, kindness, humility, meekness, longsuffering; bearing with one another, and forgiving one another, if anyone has a complaint against another; even as Christ forgave you, so you also must do. But above all these things put on love, which is the bond of perfection. And let the peace of God rule in your hearts, to which also you were called in one body; and be thankful. Let the word of Christ dwell in you richly in all wisdom, teaching and admonishing one another in psalms and hymns and spiritual songs, singing with grace in your hearts to the Lord. And whatever you do in word or deed, do all in the name of the Lord Jesus, giving thanks to God the Father through Him (Colossians 3:12–17).

If we live in the Spirit, let us also walk in the Spirit (Galatians 5:25).

Needs are all around us, both in the world and in the Church. Therefore, all of us could do many good things. We all need to know our gifts and our callings from God. We discover those as we learn to listen to His Holy Spirit. As we grow in God and in the knowledge of His Word and the principles of His Word, we discover what He is equipping us to do. To discover our gifts and callings, we may need to try some different things, but gradually it becomes clear. The passion in our hearts will direct us to where and how we should be serving God.

If we listen for His voice, He will tell us. Then our lives become much more orderly than if we do all kinds of things, not knowing where we really fit. As we seek the Lord, we discover which members of the Body of Christ we really are.

Even when we do discover our gifts and strengths given by the Holy Spirit, we need to walk in line with God's Holy Spirit. He has a path laid out for us to walk on, and we need to stay on that path. As long as we are doing that, there will be peace in our hearts. Our gifts must be under the rule of God's Holy Spirit so that we are doing His will and not the will of other people.

Sometimes compassionate and mercy-motivated people are sidetracked by the needs they see instead of walking in line with what God's Holy Spirit is saying to them. Our Heavenly Father wants to lead us by His Holy Spirit, not by needs alone. If we do not learn to follow Him, we will often be used by people instead of being used by God to do His will. Serving God involves serving people. The difference is in who is initiating it.

If the Lord leads a person to go clean someone else's house or cook a meal and the person obeys Him, he or she is serving God and walking in line with the Holy Spirit. On the other hand, if someone who is undisciplined in cleaning his or her own house hears that the person cleans houses for others as a free service and decides to take advantage of that, then the gift of helps or mercy is being used by people instead of God. We may become very tired and even resentful if we do not recognize these things. It will benefit all of us to learn to know the difference.

Romans 8:16 says, "*The Spirit Himself bears witness with our spirit that we are children of God.*" In the same way, the Holy Spirit bears witness in our spirit when we are walking in line with His plan for us.

When something churns on the inside of us when we are doing what we think is "the will of God," often the Holy Spirit is alerting us that something is not right. We need to heed that, because that is how we learn. When we heed that, usually understanding follows, even if we did not understand it initially. As we obey, more light comes. God brings people into our lives as Christians so that we can minister to them in whatever capacity He has equipped us. However, sometimes the enemy capitalizes on our good intentions and compassion and desire to serve God, and he brings people into our lives whom we cannot really help but are merely wasting our time and draining us of our energy. We need to be wise and discerning so that we are not caught in the very subtle traps that Satan sets up for us.

The difference is whether God is initiating it or not. That is why it is so important to hear from God ourselves and to discern what is going on in certain situations. Jesus sought the face of the Father to determine the path He was to follow each day, and we need to do the same.

When we serve God and obey Him, it is a joy, even if we get tired. If we end up being used by people instead of being directed by the Holy Spirit, we will lose that joy and feel confused and drained—and perhaps even burn out if we are not careful.

I encourage you to seek the Lord, discover your gifts, and obey Him with your whole life. Service to God sets you free, while doing everything people expect you to do makes you a slave to man. One brings the fear of God, which is the beginning of wisdom, and the other originates with fear of man, which brings a snare into your lives.

Pray this prayer for spiritual wisdom for yourself. Paul told the people at Ephesus he was praying this for them:

> *Therefore I also, after I heard of your faith in the Lord Jesus and your love for all the saints, do not cease to give thanks for*

you, making mention of you in my prayers: that the God of our Lord Jesus Christ, the Father of glory, may give to you the spirit of wisdom and revelation in the knowledge of Him, the eyes of your understanding being enlightened; that you may know what is the hope of His calling, what are the riches of the glory of His inheritance in the saints, and what is the exceeding greatness of His power toward us who believe, according to the working of His mighty power which He worked in Christ when He raised Him from the dead and seated Him at His right hand in the heavenly places, far above all principality and power and might and dominion, and every name that is named, not only in this age but also in that which is to come. And He put all things under His feet, and gave Him to be head over all things to the church, which is His body, the fullness of Him who fills all in all (Ephesians 1:15–23).

And whatever you do in word or deed, do all in the name of the Lord Jesus, giving thanks to God the Father through Him (Colossians 3:17).

A True Servant of the Living God

Jesus gave a picture of a true and faithful servant in a parable:

"For the kingdom of heaven is like a man traveling to a far country, who called his own servants and delivered his goods to them. And to one he gave five talents, to another two, and to another one, to each according to his own ability; and immediately he went on a journey. Then he who had received the five talents went and traded with them, and made another five talents. And likewise he who had received two gained two more also. But he who had received one went and dug in the ground, and hid his lord's money. After a long time the lord of those servants came and settled accounts with them. So he who had received five talents came and brought five other talents, saying, 'Lord, you delivered to me five talents; look, I have gained five more talents besides them.' His lord said to him, 'Well done, good and faithful servant; you were faithful over a few things, I will make you ruler over many things. Enter into the joy of your lord.' He also who had received two talents came and said, 'Lord, you delivered to me two talents; look, I have gained two more talents besides them.' His lord said to him, 'Well done, good and faithful servant; you have been faithful over a few things, I will make you ruler over many things. Enter into the joy of your lord.' Then he who had received the one talent came and said,

'Lord, I knew you to be a hard man, reaping where you have not sown, and gathering where you have not scattered seed. And I was afraid, and went and hid your talent in the ground. Look, there you have what is yours.' But his lord answered and said to him, 'You wicked and lazy servant, you knew that I reap where I have not sown, and gather where I have not scattered seed. So you ought to have deposited my money with the bankers, and at my coming I would have received back my own with interest. So take the talent from him, and give it to him who has ten talents. For to everyone who has, more will be given, and he will have abundance; but from him who does not have, even what he has will be taken away. And cast the unprofitable servant into the outer darkness. There will be weeping and gnashing of teeth'" (Matthew 25:14–30).

Jesus is speaking:

"As the Father loved Me, I also have loved you; abide in My love. If you keep My commandments, you will abide in My love, just as I have kept My Father's commandments and abide in His love. These things I have spoken to you, that My joy may remain in you, and that your joy may be full. This is My commandment, that you love one another as I have loved you. Greater love has no one than this, than to lay down one's life for his friends. You are My friends if you do whatever I command you. No longer do I call you servants, for a servant does not know what his master is doing; but I have called you friends, for all things that I heard from My Father I have made known to you" (John 15:9–15).

A loyal, faithful servant who obeys his or her master's instructions becomes a true friend. They are trustworthy, and the master can entrust them with more and more responsibility and even share secrets with them. He tells them things that His Father has told Him, and He does not make that known to everyone who is a servant, only to those who have become His friends.

A faithful and trustworthy servant takes his master's words to heart and does not neglect the instructions but follows them diligently. As the servant and master develop their relationship, trust grows between them. While the servant is learning to trust the master's character and becomes more and more loyal and dedicated to pleasing that master, the master is also observing, to see how much He can trust that servant with.

A careless or slothful servant does not follow instructions but finds his own way out, as though he knows better and has the right to do that. God wants us to follow the instructions He gives us and to use the talents He gives to each of us too. How can something given to us develop if we never exercise it or invest it to serve its purpose?

As we are able to see in the parable, He does not want us to reason it out ourselves; He wants us to make the most of what He gives us. If we do not value what He gives us, how can we expect Him to give us more? Sometimes when gifts are not operating in our lives as we would like them to, we need to examine our lives to see if we are burying the talents we already have. New ones are not going to start flowing from our lives until we are obedient with what we already have.

It is much easier to work with someone who is willing to follow instructions than with someone who always has a mind of his or her own and does not want to learn. Before we can be teachers, we must be good students. Students have to follow instructions. Effective teachers have the responsibility to lead by example and understand and follow instructions before they can instruct others. We cannot rule over many things if we have never proven to the

Master that we can be trusted to lead over one thing, a small thing. The small responsibilities entrusted to us are the seeds of the bigger responsibilities. They reproduce in appropriate proportions. If you are faithful and loyal to the first thing God trusts you with, there is no doubt that He will entrust you with greater responsibilities.

Why would a creative God give more seed to a waster? Why would He keep trying to use someone who refuses to yield or is always making excuses about why his or her skills, talents, and gifts could not be employed in the kingdom of heaven here on earth? Why would an efficient Master keep trying to use them if they are not willing to do it *His* way? When He sees one who is careful to show reverence and respect for instructions and to use the talents or gifts for the purpose the Master intended them, He will give them more.

Jesus said we are His friends if we do whatever He asks us to do. As a relationship grows between a master and servant and mutual love, respect, and trust is the result, it is no longer just a master-and-servant relationship but a friendship.

Friends share secrets, and they enjoy each other's company. They have common goals and work together. They have mutual love for the Father's will. God's Word is their only standard. They put His will first, and that is how God knows they love Him. Jesus said if we love Him, we will obey His commandments, just as He obeyed His Father's commandments to Him.

Strength

And lest I should be exalted above measure by the abundance of the revelations, a thorn in the flesh was given to me, a messenger of Satan to buffet me, lest I be exalted above measure. Concerning this thing I pleaded with the Lord three times that it might depart from me. And He said to me, "My grace is sufficient for you, for My strength is made perfect in weakness." Therefore most gladly I will rather boast in my infirmities, that the power of Christ may rest upon me. Therefore I take pleasure in infirmities, in reproaches, in needs, in persecutions, in distresses, for Christ's sake. For when I am weak, then I am strong (2 Corinthians 12:7–10).

I will love You, O LORD, my strength. The LORD is my rock and my fortress and my deliverer; My God, my strength, in whom I will trust; My shield and the horn of my salvation, my stronghold. I will call upon the LORD, who is worthy to be praised; So shall I be saved from my enemies (Psalm 18:1–3).

THE LORD is my light and my salvation; Whom shall I fear? The LORD is the strength of my life; Of whom shall I be afraid? (Psalm 27:1).

Blessed be the LORD, Because He has heard the voice of my supplications! The LORD is my strength and my shield; My heart trusted in Him, and I am helped; Therefore my heart greatly rejoices, And with my song I will praise Him (Psalm 28:6–7).

God is our refuge and strength, A very present help in trouble. Therefore we will not fear, Even though the earth be removed, And though the mountains be carried into the midst of the sea; Though its waters roar and be troubled, Though the mountains shake with its swelling. Selah There is a river whose streams shall make glad the city of God, The holy place of the tabernacle of the Most High (Psalm 46:1–4).

My flesh and my heart fail; But God is the strength of my heart and my portion forever. For indeed, those who are far from You shall perish; You have destroyed all those who desert You for harlotry. But it is good for me to draw near to God; I have put my trust in the Lord GOD, That I may declare all Your works (Psalm 73:26–28).

When we do not know what to do next and we are powerless in ourselves to change things that desperately need to be changed, we know that we have to draw strength from God. We feel weak, and we long for strength to make the necessary changes.

As followers of Jesus Christ, we know that we must call on the name of Jesus and ask Him to give us strength and give us wisdom and direction. We know we cannot do it on our own, but we are confident that we belong to the One who is all-powerful. His strength never wanes and never fades or weakens, because He is always and forever the same. Hebrews 13:8 says, *"Jesus Christ is the same yesterday, today, and forever."*

The circumstances in our lives do not cause the Lord Jesus to waver. He stays the same, and He is never powerless or weak against anything, anyone, or any forces of darkness that come against us from the satanic realm. God the Father gave Him the name Jesus, and that name is above every name. Every knee will one day bow to that name, on earth and in heaven and hell, and every tongue will confess that Jesus Christ is Lord, to the glory of God the Father (Philippians 2:9–11).

When we see things that are wrong, sinful, and very unpleasant to live with, we feel weak. Our knees weaken when we feel afraid. When things happen that we have no control over, we often despair and we worry and fret. We feel weak in such times, but when we feel weak and we know we cannot change anything, God's strength begins to come into our weaknesses and replace them with His power.

When we feel confident in our own abilities and we have—or think we have—the power to change the situation ourselves, we do not depend on God alone. When we feel powerless, we are in a perfect position for God to show His strength and glorify His name. Paul referred to something going on in his life as *"a thorn in the flesh"* (2 Corinthians 12:7). Though we would like to know exactly what that was, we do not have any evidence, but it did keep Paul in a position of having to depend on God. Something was happening to him that he was not able to overcome. It appears that Paul needed to call on God all the time to be able to cope with it. God did not just deliver him from it so that he could go on and be free of it permanently.

There has been confusion about what it meant and why God answered Paul the way He did. Paul gives us the reason for God's answer: *"lest I should be exalted above measure by the abundance of the revelations."* That is the reason God did not remove the trouble from him. God was perfecting His strength by demonstrating it in contrast to Paul's weakness.

That simply means God was bringing Paul to maturity in his trust in God. God wanted him to understand fully that we as human beings have no right to be proud and boast about things God shows us, because they are not of ourselves; they are from God. We do not have overcoming power or strength without God's power working in and through us. It is about what He is doing and what His purpose is in it all. It is not for us to look great but for God to be exalted, because the power and strength belong to Him.

When God gives us revelation of truth, it is not for us to become puffed up with what we know but for us to become like Jesus in nature. Jesus said that without Him we could do nothing (John 15:5). God wants us to understand that we have nothing to boast about except what He has done. The victory and the glory belong to God alone. We have no power unless it is His power or strength working in and through us.

When we are weak in the flesh, we become more sensitive and alert to what is going on in the spiritual realm. We are more sensitive to the voice of the Holy Spirit. It is the same as when we fast: the flesh becomes subdued, and we tune in much easier to the Spirit of God.

In the psalms quoted, we read repeatedly that strength belongs to our God. He is our strength, He is our refuge, He is our Rock, and He will show His strength when we are weak. Then He is glorified. It points people to Him and not to us.

Sometimes He allows things to stay in our lives for a while. The reason may be that He is teaching us to be dependent on Him and to understand that without Him we are helpless and weak to overcome the things that are trouble for us.

Let us not be discouraged though and think that everything we find difficult in life is meant to stay the way it is so that we will not exalt ourselves. Many times God wants to set us free from things, but we need to let Him do it His way. In this way, He can demonstrate His power, and we will not in any way take any credit for the victory but learn to draw strength and become entirely dependent on God.

Sometimes God has to bring us to the "end of ourselves" before we surrender fully so that His strength can flow through us. We must draw strength from Him regularly.

Our strength comes from Him, and He replenishes it as we wait on Him. He fills us afresh whenever we wait in His presence. Then we soar like eagles above the storm clouds. We begin to see the way He wants us to, and we draw strength for each day from Him. "*But those who wait on the LORD Shall renew their strength; They shall mount up with wings like eagles, They shall run and not be weary, They shall walk and not faint*" (Isaiah 40:31).

Hope

For I know the thoughts that I think toward you, says the LORD, thoughts of peace and not of evil, to give you a future and a hope (Jeremiah 29:11).

But I do not want you to be ignorant, brethren, concerning those who have fallen asleep, lest you sorrow as others who have no hope. For if we believe that Jesus died and rose again, even so God will bring with Him those who sleep in Jesus. For this we say to you by the word of the Lord, that we who are alive and remain until the coming of the Lord will by no means precede those who are asleep. For the Lord Himself will descend from heaven with a shout, with the voice of an archangel, and with the trumpet of God. And the dead in Christ will rise first. Then we who are alive and remain shall be caught up together with them in the clouds to meet the Lord in the air. And thus we shall always be with the Lord. Therefore comfort one another with these words (1 Thessalonians 4:13–18).

Therefore, having been justified by faith, we have peace with God through our Lord Jesus Christ, through whom also we have access by faith into this grace in which we stand, and rejoice in hope of the glory of God. And not only that, but we also glory in tribulations, knowing that tribulation produces perseverance; and perseverance, character; and character, hope. Now hope does not disappoint, because the love of God has been poured out in our hearts by the Holy Spirit who was given to us (Romans 5:1–5).

When we go through difficult times—be it sickness and pain, sorrow and grief, financial pressures, hurt and rejection, broken relationships, or whatever might befall us—we are never without hope if we put our trust in God. He is the God of all hope.

If we turn our hearts and prayers toward heaven, God hears us. He will not leave us alone or forsake us. We know what He promised, and now we have that hope. When troubles come our way, we can look to God, knowing that if we persevere and put our trust in God, He will produce His character in us because of it.

Moreover, character produces hope. When we go through fiery trials and our character is refined, the hope within us grows stronger that we will receive what God has promised if we persevere. We do not end up disappointed, because the Holy Spirit pours God's love into us, and He will not disappoint us. Whatever He does is for our own good.

Sometimes we use the word *hope* more as though it meant "wish." I hope it does not rain, or I hope it does not hurt, or I hope bad things will not happen to us. The *hope* of the Bible is not a *maybe* or a *wish*. It means something that is certain. It is certain that we will produce godly character if we persevere in the things of God. It is certain that we will not be disappointed because of that hope in the God who never changes. His Word is true, and it cannot fail. It will do what it says if we abide in Jesus and let those words of Jesus abide in us.

The Word of God says we do not sorrow as those who have no hope. It does not say we do not sorrow at all. When a loved one who is a Christian passes away, we do sorrow, and we grieve, but not as though it is the end and we will never see them again. The truth is, we will see them again. They are with Jesus. We will surely meet them when the Lord descends from heaven with a shout and with the voice of an archangel. The trumpet of God will sound. The Bible says Jesus when He comes will bring all those with Him who are already with Him or *"sleep in Jesus."* We will have a great reunion when we all meet together in the clouds in the air. After that, we will all be together and with the Lord forever. That is a marvelous hope, and it is sure.

The Lord has good plans for us, to give us a future and a hope. We already have the hope, and we know the future is a bright one because God Himself promised that He has good plans for all those who belong to Him.

Be encouraged that God has a glorious future and a hope in store for each one of you. You will receive the rewards in heaven for everything you did as unto the Lord while you lived on this earth. Often the blessings come in this life as well. To the greatest extent, the rewards await us in heaven. This life is but a vapor compared with eternal life in heaven. Great rewards are waiting for all who look forward to Christ's appearing. At that time, He will take us home to be with Him forever in all the glory and splendor of His Majestic Presence. Jesus said in His Father's house are many mansions. He went there to prepare a place for us. He is now preparing a place for us so that we can go to the same place He went when He ascended into heaven after His mission on earth was finished (John 14:2–3).

Silence

Let your conduct be without covetousness; be content with such things as you have. For He Himself has said, "I will never leave you nor forsake you" (Hebrews 13:5).

Through the LORD's mercies we are not consumed, Because His compassions fail not. They are new every morning; Great is Your faithfulness. "The LORD is my portion," says my soul, "Therefore I hope in Him!" The LORD is good to those who wait for Him, To the soul who seeks Him (Lamentations 3:22–25).

Sometimes God is silent when we want Him to speak. When He is silent, we have to examine ourselves, with God's help, to see if we have done the last thing He asked us to do. If we have, the "silence of God" means He is very pleased with what we are doing right then. He has nothing more to say to us at the time. We are in the place He wants us to be, and we are doing what He wants us to do. He is enjoying our fellowship and does not want us to fret or strive to get Him to speak. We should just enjoy the silence of His presence. When something is wrong or we need direction, He will let us know. He is our Father. He is watching over us all the time. He gives His angels charge over us.

It is a different matter when He is not answering because He is waiting to get our attention in a certain area. Sometimes He withholds an answer because we have not done something He asked us to do. Maybe without realizing it we want to bypass what He is saying. It will not work. We need to know that and acknowledge it, and we must obey. After we take care of what we should have, then we will feel His presence again.

When we ignore what He says, He does not leave us. He has promised to never leave us nor forsake us. However, we will have a sense that something is not right and we are not hearing from God as a result. When we get back on track with what He is waiting for us to do, He will give us the affirmation we need in some way so that we know all is well again.

The silence is not something to fear, but when it is God's face shining on you, and it is a sign that He is pleased with you, it is something to cherish. As you grow in the knowledge of God and in the power of His resurrection, you will also share in some of the fellowship of His sufferings. You will begin to understand all these things as you grow in your intimate love relationship with our Heavenly Father. You will begin to understand the deep things of God, which can only come through your own times and walk with Him. Someone else cannot teach you or make you experience this; it comes between you and Him. You experience fellowship with Jesus through the indwelling presence of the Holy Spirit in your life.

Pearls

Finally, brethren, whatever things are true, whatever things are noble, whatever things are just, whatever things are pure, whatever things are lovely, whatever things are of good report, if there is any virtue and if there is anything praiseworthy—meditate on these things (Philippians 4:8).

One day the Spirit of God said this to me: "Seeds of adversity, appropriately responded to, will produce a harvest of pearls." A pearl as we know it is a jewel. In this context, pearls are virtues. When adversity comes and we respond by trusting God and seeking His face to find the right way to handle it and how to respond, the result is pearls of wisdom, pearls of truth, pearls of character, and virtues of intrinsic value that produce moral excellence in our lives.

We need to act wisely and not hastily when sudden adversity comes, perhaps from unexpected places, circumstances, or people. We must not do anything rash or impulsive. The pain may last a while, and we might feel pressure to find a way out, but we must always seek the Lord and ask for His help, strength, and wisdom. When we do, He will help us, give us wisdom, and direct our lives. He will make a way through and out of the situation if we wait for Him to show us the right way to handle it.

My brethren, count it all joy when you fall into various trials, knowing that the testing of your faith produces patience. But let patience have its perfect work, that you may be perfect and complete, lacking nothing. If any of you lacks wisdom, let him ask of God, who gives to all liberally and without reproach, and it will be given to him (James 1:2–5).

If we act impetuously, we will cause more misery and suffering for ourselves. If we patiently wait on God, even when that is difficult, in the end we will reap what we have sown. If we sow to our flesh, we will reap from the flesh. However, if we listen for God's voice and we apply the principles of the Word of God to the situation, we reap a harvest of pearls instead of a harvest of weeds.

Often we do not have control over things that happen to us in this life. We always have a choice in what our response will be to what happens to us. That gives us power over situations that could otherwise overtake us and lead us into disaster. When we respond with wisdom and let the Holy Spirit guide us through our problems and adversities, it will produce godly character and virtue in us. We will grow in character and the knowledge of God, and we will reap a righteous harvest.

God's Word shows us how we need to think. Good character and right conduct begin in our thinking. When we think rightly, according to God's Word, and we make choices to obey that Word, it will result in right conduct. It will produce a harvest of righteousness and virtue—something of value that is worth the pain of discipline that was its seed.

Meditation and Studying

Oh, how I love Your law! It is my meditation all the day. You, through Your commandments, make me wiser than my enemies; For they are ever with me. I have more understanding than all my teachers, For Your testimonies are my meditation. I understand more than the ancients, Because I keep Your precepts (Psalm 119:97–100).

Remind them of these things, charging them before the Lord not to strive about words to no profit, to the ruin of the hearers. Be diligent to present yourself approved to God, a worker who does not need to be ashamed, rightly dividing the word of truth (2 Timothy 2:14–15).

We need to meditate on God's Word all the time. We need to value it enough to make it our only standard for how we conduct our lives on a daily basis. In Joshua 1:8, God told Joshua, "*This Book of the Law shall not depart from your mouth, but you shall meditate in it day and night, that you may observe to do according to all that is written in it. For then you will make your way prosperous, and then you will have good success.*"

In order to observe everything written in God's Word, we have to study it. Sometimes meditation is a difficult word for people and they do not really know what to do with it. It means to think deeply about it. That means we have to take it seriously and not forget what we read but apply it to our lives. The quoted Scripture from 2 Timothy says to be diligent to present ourselves approved to God. That means to study God's Word enough to teach it and apply it correctly—the way God intended us to understand it. He wants His servants to teach it accurately and clearly so there will be no confusion about what it means.

In order to meditate, try studying the Word of God instead of just reading it. Get a study Bible and look at the cross references to make yourself look more deeply into the meaning of what you are reading. It will help you to get it into your heart and into your mind. When you study, you think about it more than if you just read. Ask yourself what it is saying, what that means for you, and how you should use it to help others. As you do this, you will meditate on it and learn to understand and represent the truth, as God told Joshua to do.

Knowledge

Simon Peter, a bondservant and apostle of Jesus Christ, To those who have obtained like precious faith with us by the righteousness of our God and Savior Jesus Christ: Grace and peace be multiplied to you in the knowledge of God and of Jesus our Lord, as His divine power has given to us all things that pertain to life and godliness, through the knowledge of Him who called us by glory and virtue, by which have been given to us exceedingly great and precious promises, that through these you may be partakers of the divine nature, having escaped the corruption that is in the world through lust. But also for this very reason, giving all diligence, add to your faith virtue, to virtue knowledge, to knowledge self-control, to self-control perseverance, to perseverance godliness, to godliness brotherly kindness, and to brotherly kindness love. For if these things are yours and abound, you will be neither barren nor unfruitful in the knowledge of our Lord Jesus Christ (2 Peter 1:1–8).

Peter warns the people to beware of false teachers and their false doctrines. One of the false doctrines he may be referring to is Gnosticism, which taught that the way to God is through knowledge and that it is only available to the so-called elite. This of course is ludicrous.

Peter makes it very clear to them that the only way to God is through the knowledge of Jesus Christ. It is through knowing Jesus Christ and knowing the Bible that we can separate the true knowledge of God from the false religions and doctrines that rise up. It is the same today.

Knowledge, in and of itself, is nothing more than that! It will take no one to heaven. It is the knowledge of the Lord Jesus Christ and our relationship with Him that equips us to know the difference. If we have a relationship with Jesus Christ, then we know the Father as well. Jesus is the way, the truth, and the life. He Himself said so in John 14:6–7: *"Jesus said to him, 'I am the way, the truth, and the life. No one comes to the Father except through Me. If you had known Me, you would have known My Father also; and from now on you know Him and have seen Him.'"*

Jesus is the very life of God, and He dwells in our hearts by His Spirit. We become a brand new creation when we invite Jesus to dwell in us by His Spirit. Our spirit is born anew, and that is where God by His Holy Spirit dwells. We are His temple. As the nature and character of Jesus grows in us, we become more like Him and less and less the way we used to be.

Our best defense against false teachers and their doctrines is the truth. We receive revelation of truth when we receive Jesus as Savior and Lord. The Holy Spirit bears witness in our spirits that we are living in His truth. He is the truth. The knowledge that includes insight into divine truth guards us against anything false. That comes through a personal relationship with God and from reading the Bible.

We need to know Him and know His Word. They are the protection against anything that is false, deceptive, and misleading. Romans 8:16–17 says, *"The Spirit Himself bears witness with our spirit that we are children of God, and if children, then heirs—heirs of God and joint heirs with Christ, if indeed we suffer with Him, that we may also be glorified together."*

So read, study, and meditate on God's Word. Spend time with Him and invite Him to open your understanding to His Word. Get to know Him intimately. If you have a good foundation in God's Word and you know Him personally, you are in the truth. Knowledge of the truth and receiving it into our hearts and confessing it saves us; knowledge alone will not save anyone. It is in knowing Jesus, who is the truth.

Principles

You have commanded us To keep Your precepts diligently (Psalm 119:4).

Consider how I love Your precepts; Revive me, O LORD, according to Your lovingkindness (Psalm 119:159).

According to Funk and Wagnall's dictionary, the word *precept* means a rule prescribing a particular kind of conduct or action; a proverbial standard or guide to morals; a maxim. A maxim is a brief statement of a general principle, truth, or rule of conduct. A principle is a general truth or law basic to other truths, or moral standards collectively.

When the Word of God becomes the focus of our lives, it is first nature to us to apply those principles to every decision we make. It is more than following instructions. Anyone can follow an instruction, but we need to know how someone thinks or feels in order to apply their principles to our personal lives and decisions.

A principle is a general rule based on God's character and His Word that will guide us into making choices of integrity. Though many times we need to take action and there is not a specific instruction in God's Word to read, we always know the principles and precepts of the God we honor and want to glorify, and so we apply what we know and then decide. When we know Him and how He thinks, we start to think in harmony with Him. We can know the mind of Christ and find "the heart of God" in certain matters. This happens through knowing Him intimately and spending time with Him and in His Word.

These are principles of character, morality, and integrity upon which we base our lives and make our decisions every day. In order to apply the principles and obey the precepts, we have to know what they are, and we have to know the one who inspired those writings of God's Word. Second Timothy 3:16–17 says, "*All Scripture is given by inspiration of God, and is profitable for doctrine, for reproof, for correction, for instruction in righteousness, that the man of God may be complete, thoroughly equipped for every good work.*" The word *inspiration* literally means "God-breathed."

Knowing our God and applying His Word to situations in all of life is much more than being able to follow instructions. We are learning how to apply the Word of God to everything we face each day on this earth. This only comes through knowing Him and knowing His Word.

Reputation

Therefore if there is any consolation in Christ, if any comfort of love, if any fellowship of the Spirit, if any affection and mercy, fulfill my joy by being like-minded, having the same love, being of one accord, of one mind. Let nothing be done through selfish ambition or conceit, but in lowliness of mind let each esteem others better than himself. Let each of you look out not only for his own interests, but also for the interests of others. Let this mind be in you which was also in Christ Jesus, who, being in the form of God, did not consider it robbery to be equal with God, but made Himself of no reputation, taking the form of a bondservant, and coming in the likeness of men. And being found in appearance as a man, He humbled Himself and became obedient to the point of death, even the death of the cross. Therefore God also has highly exalted Him and given Him the name which is above every name, that at the name of Jesus every knee should bow, of those in heaven, and of those on earth, and of those under the earth, and that every tongue should confess that Jesus Christ is Lord, to the glory of God the Father (Philippians 2:1–11).

Self-ambition and strife are rooted in pride. People want recognition, and they want everyone else to know they are important, that they are "somebody." They love to hear their names exalted and to receive accolades, but those are fleeting experiences. They only produce satisfaction as long as the moment lasts, and then people are looking for more. They will never bring contentment. They are the opposite of humility.

Jesus willingly laid down His reputation. Jesus chose to give up the privileges and the glory He had with His Father in heaven and came to earth in the form of a human being—a baby in a manger! He emptied Himself of the privileges God Himself has, because in fact, Jesus is God the Son. John 14:9–11 says,

> *Jesus said to him, "Have I been with you so long, and yet you have not known Me, Philip? He who has seen Me has seen the Father; so how can you say, 'Show us the Father'? Do you not believe that I am in the Father, and the Father in Me? The words that I speak to you I do not speak on My own authority; but the Father who dwells in Me does the works. Believe Me that I am in the Father and the Father in Me, or else believe Me for the sake of the works themselves."*

In John 10:30 Jesus said, *"I and My Father are one."*

Your reputation is the general estimation in which people who know you or know of you hold you. When people have done great things, those who know that or recognize and appreciate that hold them in high regard. People may have a reputation for their honesty, integrity, accomplishments, or other virtues they possess. How many are willing to lay down their reputation to obey God if that is necessary? Sometimes it is.

What God thinks of us is more important than what people think of us. That is a difficult thing for many, but Jesus emptied Himself of all the privileges and the glory and laid down His reputation. He died as a common criminal. He became obedient to the death of the cross.

Life was often unpleasant for Him. The forty days of temptation in the wilderness, the rejection, the persecution, and ultimately the agony in the Garden of Gethsemane leading to death on the cross would not have been an easy time for Him. He willingly laid it all down to obey His Father.

What about us? How willing are we to lay down our reputations? We are very concerned with our reputations, but Jesus put His Father's plan first, and He laid everything else aside. Though He laid down His reputation, He did not lay down His deity. He was God in human form, come to earth to be the sinless One to die for all. We need to learn to obey and to put the interests of God ahead of our own. Otherwise, we become like the Pharisees, who loved the praise of men more than the praise of God.

When we put the interests of God ahead of our own, there will be times when we also have to put the interests of other people ahead of our own. Our lives should reflect Jesus' example. He never exercised His own rights or drew attention to Himself. He always pointed people to His Father. He said He did only what His Father showed Him. He came for the benefit of others entirely. It cost Him His reputation, but in the end, His Father exalted Him and gave Him the Name that is above every name in heaven, earth, and under the earth.

His name is His reputation. His name is indicative of who He is, what He does, and His love, mercy, grace, and power. He chose to take a lowly place and to die a humiliating death, and in the end God Himself exalted Him and gave Him a name that is higher than any other name in heaven and earth. He is the King of kings and the Lord of lords.

Faithfulness

Jesus told this parable:

"For the kingdom of heaven is like a man traveling to a far country, who called his own servants and delivered his goods to them. And to one he gave five talents, to another two, and to another one, to each according to his own ability; and immediately he went on a journey. Then he who had received the five talents went and traded with them, and made another five talents. And likewise he who had received two gained two more also. But he who had received one went and dug in the ground, and hid his lord's money. After a long time the lord of those servants came and settled accounts with them. So he who had received five talents came and brought five other talents, saying, 'Lord, you delivered to me five talents; look, I have gained five more talents besides them.' His lord said to him, 'Well done, good and faithful servant; you were faithful over a few things, I will make you ruler over many things. Enter into the joy of your lord.' He also who had received two talents came and said, 'Lord, you delivered to me two talents; look, I have gained two more talents besides them.' His lord said to him, 'Well done, good and faithful servant; you have been faithful over a few things, I will make you ruler over many things. Enter into the joy of your lord.' Then he who had received the one talent came and said,

'Lord, I knew you to be a hard man, reaping where you have not sown, and gathering where you have not scattered seed. And I was afraid, and went and hid your talent in the ground. Look, there you have what is yours.' But his lord answered and said to him, 'You wicked and lazy servant, you knew that I reap where I have not sown, and gather where I have not scattered seed. So you ought to have deposited my money with the bankers, and at my coming I would have received back my own with interest. So take the talent from him, and give it to him who has ten talents. For to everyone who has, more will be given, and he will have abundance; but from him who does not have, even what he has will be taken away" (Matthew 25:14–29).

It says the man or the master gave to each of the servants according to their ability. He did not give them more than they were capable of managing. He recognized their abilities and gave to each one accordingly. He saw what they were capable of doing, and he gave them something to invest so he could test them to see if they would use it wisely. Two of them did, but the third one did not.

He hid what his master gave to him, and therefore he had no harvest, no increase, and no growth in any way. He wasted the talent he had; he actually buried it. Then he told the master he could have it back. However, the master was not impressed. He did not give him more to see what the unprofitable servant would do with that. He gave orders to take the talent from the one-talent person and give it to the one who had the most, because he had used his talents well. That may not sound very fair to some of us.

There is a principle in operation here. God does not expect us to use what we do not have, but He tests us to see if we will be faithful with what we have. If we are, He will give us greater responsibility. He tests us in areas where sometimes no one other than God sees what we are doing. He sees our capabilities, and He gives something to each one of us to do. We all have something to contribute in the kingdom of heaven if we are members of the body of Christ, which is His Church here on earth.

God sees when we make commitments to use our God-given gifts and abilities and then do not fulfill our commitments to that service. Often it might seem inconsequential—Who will notice if I do not show up? What difference does it make anyway?—and on it goes. When we make commitments in the areas of our gifts and abilities and someone else is counting on us to be there but we neglect to take care of those duties, it matters a great deal.

For things to function the way God intends them to do, each member has to do his or her part. If someone expects us to be in church, whether we have made a commitment to be an usher or greeter, to teach the children or to pray for others, and we do not show up to fill our commitment, we cause stress for others, and God sees our slothfulness. He rewards faithfulness, and He has no tolerance for laziness or slothfulness. Those who are faithful to their commitments will experience greater opportunities. Those who neglect their duties will receive fewer and fewer opportunities and perhaps eventually have no opportunities, because by their actions they prove themselves unfaithful.

We all need to take our God-given responsibilities seriously. When He gives us an ability or gift, He has an assignment for us in a place where that gift or talent will serve the purpose for which He gave it.

Those who are leaders or have responsibility over others in ministry or other area of life know how refreshing it is when we have faithful people working with us. It is refreshing when people say they will be there and you know you do not have to wonder about that, because you can count on them. It is truly a wonderful characteristic in people's lives. Then there are those who do not follow instructions; when they are not going to be there they do not find someone to take their places; and it causes frustration and inconvenience. Eventually you would just as soon they were not on your team at all. If that is how we feel, can we not understand that God values faithfulness? Commitment to do what He says is very important!

God promotes the faithful. He gives more opportunities to those who are already making good use of what He has given them, not to those who leave their talents and gifts dormant. God is eternally faithful, and He wants His servants to be faithful as well. Rewards await the faithful, and opportunities will come to them in this life as well. Why would God promote someone who is not using what He has given them? Why would He give someone greater responsibilities if they were not responsible or faithful to what He asked of them with less? He tests us in the small things, and if He sees we are faithful, He will increase our responsibilities.

We must be faithful to what He calls us to every day–just as He is faithful. *"Through the LORD's mercies we are not consumed, Because His compassions fail not. They are new every morning; Great is Your faithfulness"* (Lamentations 3:22–23).

Self-Control

But the fruit of the Spirit is love, joy, peace, longsuffering, kindness, goodness, faithfulness, gentleness, self-control. Against such there is no law. And those who are Christ's have crucified the flesh with its passions and desires. If we live in the Spirit, let us also walk in the Spirit (Galatians 5:22–25).

Self-control is a fruit of God's Holy Spirit. When we do not control or discipline ourselves, we practice the opposite, which is letting the "flesh," or the "carnal nature," lead us to do whatever it feels like doing. For example, if someone makes me very upset, I might feel justified to give them "a piece of my mind," as we sometimes refer to it. If I choose not to do that, and I do what is right according to God's Word by staying calm and not answering rudely or giving my opinion, that is called self-control. We may feel angry, but we must control our anger. Feeling anger is not the sin. What we do with it determines whether we sin or not.

Sometimes circumstances merit anger. If I see unrighteousness, injustice, violence, or abuse, for example, and there is not some anger in me about it, that is not normal. It is normal to feel angry at things such as those. If a man or woman finds out his or her spouse has had an affair and been unfaithful to the marriage covenant, anger is a normal reaction. Nevertheless, self-control is a choice about how we will manage that anger. When negative circumstances, and adverse conditions, trigger negative emotions in us, we have to learn to exercise self-control. Of course, this is easier to say than it is to do when it is necessary. Only as we mature spiritually and these characteristics become more and more evident in our lives can we truly recognize their value.

In times of frustration and anger, it is easy to speak words we live to regret. Words spoken in moments of exasperation and anger can do lasting damage to relationships. It is easy to speak them, but once spoken we cannot retract them. Our words have impact on the ears and the hearts that hear them, so we must control how we use them. That takes a lifetime of practice. As we become more like Jesus and the fruit of His Spirit, His own characteristics, mature in us, we learn more and more how to control our tongues and our actions in critical times. Then we will not say or do things we live to regret—at least not as often as we once did, and gradually less and less.

If we exercise self-control, it means we have learned to think of the consequences before we speak or act. It is a virtue, a pearl of great value, that we all need to cultivate in our lives. Very likely, we all have need of it every day, or at least most days. Many opportunities will come along for each of us when we could lose "our cool" and forget about self-control and cause a bigger problem. When we do exercise this virtue, it will always bring a positive reward. Even if no one else knows what you felt or what you could have said or done when the opportunity came to lose control, you will know it in your heart, and that in itself is a reward of having exercised it. It is always worth doing. We do not regret letting the fruit of the Spirit operate after we have done so. We often have regrets when we have failed to do so and gave way to our old sinful nature instead.

Take heed to God's Word. The quoted Scripture says those who are Christ's have crucified the flesh with its passions and desires. We no longer allow it to rule; we choose to let God's Holy Spirit lead us, and we obey His Word. We live in the Spirit, and we walk in the Spirit.

Excellent Spirit

Now all the king's wise men came, but they could not read the writing, or make known to the king its interpretation. Then King Belshazzar was greatly troubled, his countenance was changed, and his lords were astonished. The queen, because of the words of the king and his lords, came to the banquet hall. The queen spoke, saying, "O king, live forever! Do not let your thoughts trouble you, nor let your countenance change. There is a man in your kingdom in whom is the Spirit of the Holy God. And in the days of your father, light and understanding and wisdom, like the wisdom of the gods, were found in him; and King Nebuchadnezzar your father—your father the king—made him chief of the magicians, astrologers, Chaldeans, and soothsayers. Inasmuch as an excellent spirit, knowledge, understanding, interpreting dreams, solving riddles, and explaining enigmas were found in this Daniel, whom the king named Belteshazzar, now let Daniel be called, and he will give the interpretation" (Daniel 5:8–12).

 Daniel knew his God. God gave him the interpretations of the dreams and the interpretation of the writing on the wall.

 As Daniel's favor grew, others were envious and jealous. King Belteshazzar made him the third ruler in the kingdom. After Belteshazzar died, Darius set up three governors over his kingdom, one of which was Daniel. Daniel had distinguished himself above the others because there was an excellent spirit in him (Daniel 6:3). The other government officials devised a way to get rid of Daniel, but it did not work. They decided that the only way they would be able to find any charges against him would be to involve Daniel's faith in God. They manipulated King Darius into signing a decree forbidding anyone to petition any god or man other than King Darius for thirty days. They would cast anyone who did otherwise into a den of lions.

When Daniel knew the decree was signed he went home to his upper room, opened his window, turned his face toward Jerusalem, knelt down, and prayed three times a day, just as he had always done before. The government officials watched him and reported what they had seen—Daniel praying to his God. The king was sorry and he sought for a way to deliver Daniel, but he had signed the decree and now, even as the king, he could not reverse it. Therefore, he gave the orders and threw Daniel into the lions' den.

King Darius told Daniel that God would deliver him. Then they put a stone in front of the lions' den, and the king sealed it with his own signet ring and with the signets of his lords so that the purpose concerning Daniel might not be changed.

The king went home that night and fasted. He was unable to sleep. First thing in the morning, he went to the den of lions and called out to Daniel to ask him if he was still alive and if his God had been able to deliver him from the lions. Daniel told the king that God sent His angel to shut the lions' mouths because He found him innocent. Furthermore, Daniel told King Darius that not only did God find him innocent but also he had done nothing against the king.

The king was very happy that Daniel was not hurt, and he commanded his men to throw all those who sought to kill Daniel into the lions' den, along with their wives and their children. The lions overpowered them and crushed all their bones before they even hit the bottom of the den. After that, Daniel prospered in the reigns of both Darius and Cyprus. It went well with Daniel because he honored his God and he refused to compromise in any way. God honored him and delivered him (Daniel 6).

Daniel trusted God to save him, even in the lions' den. God shut the lions' mouths so they could not harm Daniel in any way. Daniel did not hide the fact that he prayed to only the One True God, and regardless of the persecution, he did not bow to anyone other than the One True God. He had excellent moral standards, and God continued to give him favor.

Daniel's three friends refused to worship anyone but their God, and they did not bow down to the golden image, because they refused to compromise their faith in any way. Nebuchadnezzar ordered them to be cast into the fiery furnace, and when he watched he saw a fourth man in the furnace. They were all walking around unharmed. He said the form of the fourth man was like the Son of God (Daniel 3:25). God honored and delivered them.

We likewise must not compromise what the Bible teaches. We too should be people of moral excellence and live righteously, even if people persecute us for it. If we do this, we bring glory to God, and He will honor us for it as well. We need to ask God for strength to obey Him and live according to His Word. These are opportunities to see God's grace, mercy, deliverance, protection, and provision manifested in our times of need for the supernatural as well. He is an Awesome God, and He reigns. He is an excellent God, and we need to have an excellent moral commitment to live in the integrity of God Himself too.

Time

Now it happened as they went that He entered a certain village; and a certain woman named Martha welcomed Him into her house. And she had a sister called Mary, who also sat at Jesus' feet and heard His word. But Martha was distracted with much serving, and she approached Him and said, "Lord, do You not care that my sister has left me to serve alone? Therefore tell her to help me." And Jesus answered and said to her, "Martha, Martha, you are worried and troubled about many things. But one thing is needed, and Mary has chosen that good part, which will not be taken away from her" (Luke 10:38–42).

Time is something we all have the same amount of, and yet it seems time is a scarce commodity and many people are always busy. At times they are so busy doing things "in church" that there is not time enough for the Church—the people! Often we go to church and are with many other people but we go home lonely and feeling alone. It is not biblical fellowship.

It seems there is not time for getting to know each other and showing some love, compassion, and kindness to others, because everything is "rush, rush, rush"! We rush to get to church and then we rush to perform our duties while we are at church. How many go home lonely and hurting and feeling no different when they come home from church than when they went to church?

It seems there need to be some adjustments made. Though many people talk about the busyness and how it can be the enemy of what God really wants us to do, no one is doing anything to change it. *Busy* is a word we hear often, and it seems as though people often equate busyness with being important. If someone is very busy, he or she must be in demand and therefore is a very important person. This is not necessarily true. I do not think God sees it that way. The most important thing in all of life is to use our time to do God's will and do it with all our hearts.

People have their jobs, their families, their church commitments, and they run themselves weary trying to get everything on their busy schedules done. They are trying to make sure that everyone will be satisfied. It is important that they meet everyone's expectations so they will not feel guilty. Sometimes it feels like a merry-go-round with no place to get off. Changes are needed, and we all need to seek the Lord to find out how He wants us to change. We cannot change it for everyone, but where do we start to do it for ourselves, our families, and maybe our own congregation? I believe God always has a solution if we have an ear to hear Him.

When Jesus visited Mary and Martha's home, Martha complained to Him because her sister, Mary, was not helping her serve. In fact, she asked Jesus to tell Mary to help her. Jesus took the other side. He said Mary has chosen the one good thing, which will be her portion for eternity. He said Mary chose the things that have eternal value. She sat at His feet and had fellowship with Jesus, and He taught her truth that would change her life.

When we have no time for people, we are not living the way Jesus did. In the midst of multitudes, Jesus stopped for individuals. He saw individual needs and responded accordingly. He healed entire multitudes, and He interrupted His journey to what we would say was an emergency to minister to another individual.

In three of the gospels, Matthew, Mark, and Luke, we have the story of the woman who had been bleeding for twelve years. The Bible says she had suffered many things and spent all the money she had on physicians, and she was no better. In fact, she continually got worse. She was among a multitude of people, and Jairus, a ruler of the synagogue, had just asked Jesus to come to his house because his twelve-year-old daughter was dying. It says in Luke 8:41–42 that Jairus fell down at Jesus' feet and begged him to come before his daughter died.

However, while all this was going on, the woman touched Jesus and received her healing. Jesus stopped and asked who had touched Him. He knew someone had, because He perceived that healing power left Him. The woman told Him she had touched Him and immediately the bleeding stopped. He told her to be of good cheer because her faith had made her well. He told her to go in peace.

Meanwhile, someone from Jairus' home came to tell Him not to bother going there because his daughter had died. Jesus told them not to be afraid but believe because He would heal her. They laughed at Him, but He went to their home and commanded her to "arise," and she did (Luke 8:40–56). He loved people and cared for their needs. He allowed people and their needs to interrupt His schedule. He was not too busy to minister to them.

Sometimes I think we need to do more than just use our time efficiently; we actually need to eliminate some things to make room for the things that will follow us into eternity. We need to simplify our lives by eliminating things expected of us and start doing things that will make our lives easier and happier. Relationships are very important, and we cannot cultivate them very well if we are always busy and always in a hurry to get to our next duty.

We need to stop trying to meet all the expectations of all the people and start meeting the expectations of One Master—Jesus.

When we do what He expects of us, it frees us from trying to meet all the expectations of everyone around us. In the end, we will be happier ourselves, and we will have more friends than we had when we tried to please everyone. We cannot please everyone—it just does not work that way! We cannot do everything someone asks us to do, even in church. It is important to stay within the ministry to which God has called each of us. Moreover, He does not make us too busy to care for each other. We do that to ourselves. He cares about people and makes time for them, and we should too. That is why He died for them.

We cannot meet the needs of all the people around us, but if we listen to Jesus and walk in the Spirit, we will meet the needs of the ones He wants us to touch. We only have one chance to live this life. James tells us that this life is a vapor that appears for a little time and then vanishes away (James 4:14). At the end of our lives, it will be our relationship with Jesus and the people we love, the relationships we cultivated in this life and how we treated each other, that will have true meaning and value. We may wish we had given more time to people instead of other things.

Disappointment

Now hope does not disappoint, because the love of God has been poured out in our hearts by the Holy Spirit who was given to us (Romans 5:5).

Sometimes we have our hopes up for something wonderful to happen, and when it does not, we are disappointed. At one time or another in this life, every one of us will face some kind of disappointment. When it happens to us, what should we do?

Maybe we blame ourselves for something we did that caused us to be very disappointed in ourselves. On the other hand, maybe something completely beyond our control happened and we ended up very disappointed. Whatever the cause, we have to examine it, acknowledge the facts, and try to move on past it. It seems like the end of the world, but usually it is not.

Depending on how deep the disappointment is, we have to allow ourselves time to get over it. If we did something wrong and it cost us something big, we have to allow ourselves time to grieve the loss. Regardless of whether the loss is big or small, we have to choose to look at the other side. When we get over it, or at least get past the initial shock of it, what did we learn from it, or at least what should we learn from it? We have to evaluate it realistically. Whether it was our own doing or something we had no control over, we have to let go of it in time and then ask God to teach us from it and bring good out of it.

When you are touched by one of the irritations of life, ask the Lord to bring forth a pearl from it. Choose to grow better and not bitter from your disappointments in life. Turn them into learning experiences so that instead of always remembering it with bitterness, you can value the pearl you now have in your life and take with you as you move forward. Instead of rehearsing the irritation, carry the gem and brighten someone else's life with the virtue and fruit of the Spirit growing in your life.

Turn your disappointments into victories by refusing to give up. Press on toward the goal for the prize of your high calling (Philippians 3:14). You can triumph through all your problems when Christ is at the center of your life. You are not alone. He knows what is happening, and He cares. He will turn your sorrows into joy (John 16:20) and give you beauty for ashes and the oil of joy for mourning and a garment of praise instead of a spirit of heaviness (Isaiah 61:3).

The Holy Spirit has poured God's love into our hearts, and we know that even though we face disappointments in life, God's love does not change and He is with us, and we will see the promises of God fulfilled in our lives if we trust in Him.

Depression

Now David was greatly distressed, for the people spoke of stoning him, because the soul of all the people was grieved, every man for his sons and his daughters. But David strengthened himself in the LORD his God (1 Samuel 30:6).

This is not referring to clinical depression, which clearly requires the expertise of medical professionals. They are the ones who know how to treat such conditions. They decide when it is necessary.

However, from time to time many of us have circumstances in our lives that depress us. Sometimes we have a problem we do not have the answers to. We may experience feelings of helplessness and hopelessness, and yet when we know Jesus, deep within us is a hope that He can change things. Sometimes we don't understand why He has not done that yet, and the part of us that doubts wonders if He really will.

During these times, we lack vitality and our spirits are low. Our joy is sadly lacking. The sadness, weariness, and the stress of it sap the life and energy from our lives. Our joy is gone, and we feel desperate for encouragement, which gives us hope again. This is the time to persevere, exercise our faith, and choose to apply the Word of God to our lives and circumstances, whether they seem hopeless or not.

It takes faith to do this, but when we continue to trust in the Lord, in the end we will experience victory over our negative emotions caused by adverse circumstances. God will bring a solution in His way and at the right time, if we determine to do the will of God even when circumstances are not easy. During these times, we must decide to apply God's Word to our lives and exercise our faith regardless of how we feel in those circumstances.

In 1 Samuel 30 we find the account of the Amalekites attacking Ziklag when David and his men were away, being chased by Saul. The Amalekites set Ziklag on fire. They did not kill anyone, but they took them all as their captives. It says David was greatly distressed because the people who were with him threatened to stone him. They were very grieved because their families were missing, and they wept until their strength was gone and they had no more power to weep. David had no one to turn to except His God, and he strengthened and encouraged himself in the Lord. He asked for the ephod, and he asked God what he should do in this very serious situation.

The Lord answered David and told him to pursue the Amalekites. He told David they would surely overtake their enemies and recover everything. God gave them a strategy for battle, and they had a complete victory. First Samuel 30:19 says, *"And nothing of theirs was lacking, either small or great, sons or daughters, spoil or anything which they had taken from them; David recovered all."*

When things are less than favorable for us, we also need to encourage ourselves with the Word of God and seek Him for the solution. Then we can say as the psalmist did in Psalm 120:1, *"In my distress I cried to the LORD, And He heard me."*

Frustration

But we have this treasure in earthen vessels, that the excellence of the power may be of God and not of us. We are hard-pressed on every side, yet not crushed; we are perplexed, but not in despair; persecuted, but not forsaken; struck down, but not destroyed—always carrying about in the body the dying of the Lord Jesus, that the life of Jesus also may be manifested in our body (2 Corinthians 4:7–10).

The things that frustrate or baffle us are the circumstances, people, or things in our lives that keep us from achieving our goals, dreams, or desires. Sometimes we have a vision from God but there are things that seem like hindrances in our way, and they seem like roadblocks to doing what we believe God wants us to do. These things can be perplexing, confusing, and discouraging, but we have to keep looking ahead and pursuing what we know God wants us to do.

Sometimes we are frustrated because we are trying to make something happen and God is trying to get our attention in another area. Maybe we think we are on the right path and we have direction, but there are times when we are wrong about things like that and we need to check with the Lord. If He is trying to get our attention and we are blaming others or circumstances instead of listening to Him, the frustrations will intensify. We need to ask the Lord about everything.

There are times when the enemy is frustrating and thwarting the plans God has for us. It is a weapon of Satan to keep us from doing the will of God. Then we need to press in, take our stand, and not give in to those obstacles but resist him and keep doing what we know is right in the eyes of God. In doing so, we are submitting to God and thereby resisting the enemy, and he has to leave us (James 4:7). We have to seek the Lord until we discern His voice in the matter, and then we will know how to move forward.

Regardless of how frustrating these things can be, God uses them to build character in our lives if we respond appropriately. Sometimes it involves timing. Maybe we have the right desires, and the vision we have is from God, but there is timing involved, and that is up to God. In the meantime, we have to exercise patience and be still and know that He is God and He will bring it to pass if we stay close to Him while we are going through the frustrating times.

Drudgery

Jesus is speaking:

"He who receives you receives Me, and he who receives Me receives Him who sent Me. He who receives a prophet in the name of a prophet shall receive a prophet's reward. And he who receives a righteous man in the name of a righteous man shall receive a righteous man's reward. And whoever gives one of these little ones only a cup of cold water in the name of a disciple, assuredly, I say to you, he shall by no means lose his reward" (Matthew 10:40–42).

Receiving someone for who they are in Christ is not a very big responsibility. Yet Jesus takes notice of those things, and He will reward everyone for every time they honor these words. To give someone a cup of cold water seems like a very menial task, but there will be a reward.

Perhaps it seems to us that prophets of God who fulfill their calling would merit a significant reward. They are prominent, and they make such a difference in the church and bring much encouragement to the body of Christ in many notable ways. We have no difficulty believing that they will have great rewards in heaven. Meanwhile many of us may be doing menial, wearisome, and even dull tasks, and we wonder if it even matters whether we keep doing those things or not. Jesus said if we receive a prophet in the name of a prophet, we would also receive a prophet's reward. That is something worth contemplating, because it can make a mundane task seem a whole lot more worthwhile.

If we expect some great thing to happen every single day of our lives, it will merely frustrate us, because for the most part this life is not like that. Every day can be meaningful and fruitful if we see it as another day to make the best of everything that comes our way. If we realize that every time we respond righteously to even an unrighteous person who mistreats us or to something unpleasant done to us there will be a reward and it is not in vain, it will take the drudgery out of everyday life and give us a heavenly perspective. In its season it will bear fruit in this life, and it will bring eternal rewards as well.

We all have our everyday drudgery, but our attitude determines the way we feel about it. If we do whatever we do with all our hearts as unto the Lord, we will feel differently about it, and furthermore, it too will bring rewards in eternity.

If we do well what our hands find to do now, God will promote us when the time is right. If we complain all the time, that will likely not happen. Remember, attitude makes all the difference.

Procrastination

He who has a slack hand becomes poor, But the hand of the diligent makes rich (Proverbs 10:4).

The hand of the diligent will rule, But the lazy man will be put to forced labor (Proverbs 12:24).

The soul of a lazy man desires, and has nothing; But the soul of the diligent shall be made rich (Proverbs 13:4).

When things we need to do seem unpleasant, the temptation is to procrastinate. That will not bring us peace, and we will not make progress in that area until we exercise some discipline and do what we know we should be doing.

People who procrastinate often have good intentions. They tell themselves they will do it tomorrow or next week or next month. When that time comes, they often give themselves an extension so they can postpone the commitments they need to take some action on. People who are habitual procrastinators are seldom successful in life, because of their tardiness. They put things off until tomorrow, and tomorrow always has another tomorrow. They lack discipline, and without any discipline, they do not succeed at much.

Some people procrastinate all the time, and others do it occasionally, but when we are tempted to do it, it is important not to let ourselves get away with it. There are times in every person's life when we need to do some things we do not enjoy. We have to do them because they are necessary for our good. The less we like something, the less we look forward to doing it. We have to bring that under control. We should not govern our lives by what we feel like doing. We have to discipline ourselves to do what we need to be doing for our own good. Sometimes it is for the good of others as well.

It is very frustrating to depend on procrastinators. They make other people's lives frustrating as well. An employer will not usually promote someone who is a procrastinator but will promote a disciplined person who will take action and get the job done, and get it done on time. When tardy people make commitments and then do not show up, they frustrate the plans of others who are depending on them.

When God tells us to do something, it is not usually up for negotiation. He expects us to do it as soon as we understand. If we do not act upon what He says but procrastinate, thinking to ourselves that we will do it eventually, He will not keep speaking to us. He has spoken to us about something, and until we stop procrastinating, He will not speak to us about new things.

Rejection

Who has believed our report? And to whom has the arm of the LORD been revealed? For He shall grow up before Him as a tender plant, And as a root out of dry ground. He has no form or comeliness; And when we see Him, There is no beauty that we should desire Him. He is despised and rejected by men, A Man of sorrows and acquainted with grief. And we hid, as it were, our faces from Him; He was despised, and we did not esteem Him (Isaiah 53:1–3).

He came to His own, and His own did not receive Him (John 1:11).

Then the soldiers of the governor took Jesus into the Praetorium and gathered the whole garrison around Him. And they stripped Him and put a scarlet robe on Him. When they had twisted a crown of thorns, they put it on His head, and a reed in His right hand. And they bowed the knee before Him and mocked Him, saying, "Hail, King of the Jews!" Then they spat on Him, and took the reed and struck Him on the head. And when they had mocked Him, they took the robe off Him, put His own clothes on Him, and led Him away to be crucified (Matthew 27:27–31).

    Those who rejected Jesus rejected the Father and thereby rejected eternal life. No one will ever suffer to the extent that Jesus did, and He had no sin to deserve any of it. The treatment He received was violent, cruel, and inhumane. He knew who He was and why He was here, so He kept His face toward heaven and worked with the Father to finish the mission and to be Savior, Redeemer, and Friend to all who would receive Him.

He said if people hated Him, they would also hate us (John 15:18–19). Those who hate righteousness and do not want to hear the truth will hate those who proclaim the truth. Great rewards are waiting in heaven for all who have suffered rejection and persecution for righteousness' sake. Many have been martyred, and they will have even greater rewards in heaven. Jesus said it is inevitable that it will happen, but it is not in vain. All who suffer for righteousness' sake will reap a harvest in heaven for it (Matthew 5:10).

That is one kind of rejection, something we cannot escape if we are openly following Jesus and obeying God's Word. In varying degrees, of course, we all experience some of this as Christians.

There are other areas in life where we struggle with rejection. People go through many hurtful things in life. Parents who fail to show proper love and affirmation to their children may cause them to suffer with a root of rejection. This is emotional and requires restoration of the soul. Some children mistreat others in school, and those feel rejected by their peers. Children and teens often suffer from deep emotional wounds if others bully them, belittle them, and laugh at them. We need to identify this for what it is to facilitate healing.

Roots produce fruit, and we have to get rid of the root and the fruit. Sometimes rebellion results from the suffering from an authority figure who abused that power. The Lord is our Shepherd, and He restores our souls, which include our wounded emotions, our tormented minds, and the rebellion in our wills.

In the case of persecution for righteousness' sake, God is our strength. The Holy Spirit is always with us to help us and give us wisdom and everything we need. There are many other kinds of rejection. It may come from a leader, a spouse, or a friend. It all hurts, and we likely will all experience it at some time.

When others reject us, our Heavenly Father embraces us. Jesus is the Friend who is closer than any other (Proverbs 18:24), and we all have Him as our refuge. He has promised never to leave us or forsake us (Hebrews 13:5–6).

Encouragement

Blessed be the God and Father of our Lord Jesus Christ, the Father of mercies and God of all comfort, who comforts us in all our tribulation, that we may be able to comfort those who are in any trouble, with the comfort with which we ourselves are comforted by God. For as the sufferings of Christ abound in us, so our consolation also abounds through Christ (2 Corinthians 1:3–5).

We may not face the same opposition, and perhaps not as severe, as Paul faced when he penned this letter to the Corinthians; however, we too face our trials, tribulations, and hardships in this life.

Our comfort and consolation come from God Himself. One of the Holy Spirit's names is Comforter. When we go through difficulties in this life, He comforts us and helps us on our way through these things. When we have come through, we have overcome that problem. When we are overcomers, we become encouragers. The things we experience ourselves are the things we can best understand and have faith for to help others overcome their hardships, discouragements, and pain as well.

If we understand this, then we know that our suffering is never in vain. If we did not cause it, we still need to have a right attitude while it is happening to us. If we brought it on ourselves through our own foolishness or bad choices, we can still learn from it and ask the Lord to bring good out of it. We need to ask God to give us wisdom and understanding so that we can triumph over the problem and come through victoriously.

Everything that happened to us can benefit or comfort others if we make that choice. We do not need to look very far to find someone who is discouraged, sick, or going through financial hardships. We all need encouragement from time to time, and it makes a big difference to just talk to people who understand and give us hope again. They do that by sharing their problems and their victories. They tell us how God comforted them, helped them, and caused them to triumph in Christ Jesus.

First Corinthians 14:1 says, "*Pursue love, and desire spiritual gifts, but especially that you may prophesy.*" Without love, it all counts for nothing. That is the most important virtue in a Christian's life. In love, we need to desire spiritual gifts and especially that we might prophesy. The gift of prophesy is for the purpose of edification, comfort, and exhortation.

It is easy to understand why the apostle Paul mentioned this gift above others in this context. The need for edifying or building up, encouragement, comfort, and exhortation is great in the Church. It is hard to motivate others to righteousness and good works when we feel discouraged and cast down ourselves. We all need to exhort each other to good works—doing the will of God. Be an encourager! You will reap a harvest of peace. Do not tear down, but build others up in the Lord! In Jesus' name, bring hope to a lost and dying world!

Presumptuousness

The law of the LORD is perfect, converting the soul; The testimony of the LORD is sure, making wise the simple; The statutes of the LORD are right, rejoicing the heart; The commandment of the LORD is pure, enlightening the eyes; The fear of the LORD is clean, enduring forever; The judgments of the LORD are true and righteous altogether. More to be desired are they than gold, Yea, than much fine gold; Sweeter also than honey and the honeycomb. Moreover by them Your servant is warned, And in keeping them there is great reward. Who can understand his errors? Cleanse me from secret faults. Keep back Your servant also from presumptuous sins; Let them not have dominion over me. Then I shall be blameless, And I shall be innocent of great transgression. Let the words of my mouth and the meditation of my heart Be acceptable in Your sight, O LORD, my strength and my Redeemer (Psalm 19:7–14).

Presumptuousness is rudeness or arrogance. Presumptuous people are often inconsiderate, disrespectful of others, and overconfident. They are foolish even to the point of doing things they are not entitled or even qualified to do. They are not cautious. They do not pray or think things through before they act.

Presumptuous people make many mistakes and seldom seek the advice of others. They presume to know better than others do.

They do not like to defer to others. Listeners always learn more than people who do not like to listen to others. It is an absence of the fear of the Lord.

They rudely push their opinions on others and try to persuade them to follow their ideas. Presumptuousness has no place in the life a believer. Presumptuous people assume they already know the best way to do things.

This is a great sin in the body of Christ. It keeps us from God's best for the Church. Presumptuousness is the enemy of faith. Many times what we hear people refer to as *faith* is nothing more than presumptuousness. Faith is not just stepping out on a limb and doing something that others might fear to do. It is confidence in God's Word, knowing God and walking in the Spirit—wherever He leads. When we walk with God, we say and do whatever He asks us to do. It is a matter of being in step with the Holy Spirit and doing whatever He tells us to do. That is living by faith. It is a sure conviction that God's Word is true and that God can be trusted.

Sometimes when God speaks and asks a person to do something, it might appear to others who have not heard that from God that the person is merely stepping out on a limb. If God ordered it, then God will support that limb, and the person will not end up looking like "a fool."

Presumptuousness means we act without wisdom and we act without actually having heard from God. He wants us to wait, because the Holy Spirit is the leader. He wants to lead the Church leaders and He wants to lead the individual believers in their everyday lives. Jesus gives His Holy Spirit to every believer, and He is with us to lead us and guide us into all truth. We need to act cautiously, and then we can move forward in confidence. In this way, there is room for God to correct us before we end up making fools of ourselves.

Strongholds

Now I, Paul, myself am pleading with you by the meekness and gentleness of Christ—who in presence am lowly among you, but being absent am bold toward you. But I beg you that when I am present I may not be bold with that confidence by which I intend to be bold against some, who think of us as if we walked according to the flesh. For though we walk in the flesh, we do not war according to the flesh. For the weapons of our warfare are not carnal but mighty in God for pulling down strongholds, casting down arguments and every high thing that exalts itself against the knowledge of God, bringing every thought into captivity to the obedience of Christ, and being ready to punish all disobedience when your obedience is fulfilled (2 Corinthians 10:1–6).

A stronghold is a fortress built to defend or protect something. It is a defensible place, a concentrated area, where certain opinions or mindsets have built a foundation solidly so they cannot easily be changed, approached, or attacked. Strongholds can be corporate or individual. Certain groups have certain mindsets, beliefs, and opinions.

They can be false doctrines, or they can be other lies people believe. Strongholds begin in the minds of people who, for whatever reason, come to believe a lie about something, someone, or some group or about himself or herself. Anything that exalts itself against God's Word and is firmly rooted in our minds is a stronghold. A stronghold is not a demon. However, a stronghold is an entry point for the demonic.

Deliverance does not come easily if people have strongholds in their minds. Behind every stronghold are a lie and a fear. Demons attach themselves to strongholds. The lie behind the stronghold is the ground that the demon is standing on. When you take away that ground, the demon has to go. He has nothing to hang on to anymore. The lies have to be exposed and then replaced with the truth. The truth is God's Word.

Flesh and blood cannot tear these down. They are places of personal bondage in people's lives that can only be torn down with the weapons God has given to the believers. They are God's Word, the Blood of Jesus shed on the cross, the name of Jesus, and God's Holy Spirit living in us.

People, especially as children, often start to believe lies about themselves. Perhaps someone who has a lot of influence over them tells them they will never succeed, they are not smart, or they are not good enough to do certain things they dream about doing. Often these things affect them very intensely as children, and even as adults those things affect people. It is hard to tell them anything different because they have believed those lies about themselves for so long. Even though it is not what God says about them, they cannot seem to stop believing the lie. It has become a stronghold in their minds.

Someone—perhaps a parent, sibling, or teacher—influenced them with that lie about themselves, and they dwelt on it until it became a stronghold. If not set free by the power of God's truth, which is His Word, they often live with their bondage throughout their whole lives, believing that lie about themselves, even though they are Christians. It can be very detrimental to their victory in living the Christian life.

Lies have to be exposed. A stronghold is a structure built around a lie. We need to discover, with the help of the Holy Spirit, how that lie started and how that door opened and how the enemy has used it against them since. Then expose it for what it is, replace it with truth, and chase the enemy away. It is a lie that has a hold on them or is holding them captive. Jesus came to set the captives free! Hallelujah!

Healthy Relationships

The Lord spoke to Joshua:

"This Book of the Law shall not depart from your mouth, but you shall meditate in it day and night, that you may observe to do according to all that is written in it. For then you will make your way prosperous, and then you will have good success" (Joshua 1:8).

Joshua said to the people:

"And if it seems evil to you to serve the LORD, choose for yourselves this day whom you will serve, whether the gods which your fathers served that were on the other side of the River, or the gods of the Amorites, in whose land you dwell. But as for me and my house, we will serve the LORD" (Joshua 24:15).

The most important relationship choice we make next to our decision to receive Jesus as Savior is who we marry. If we are Christians at the time, that should be the first criteria, that the person we marry is also a Christian. How can there be peace and harmony when two people married to each other do not agree on something this vital?

When we have children, we reproduce. We may hope to produce children who will not be the way we are and pick up our negative traits, but the process is reproduction. They will become, in many ways, like the model they see every day. We need to have the right goals for raising children. How can we raise them in the ways of the Lord if the one spouse does not agree that the Bible is God's way?

It is important to share each other's dreams and goals. Of course, some of this depends on how mature the individuals are at the time. They may not be completely clear on these matters and discover their dreams and goals later on after they have been married for some time. Certainly though, these are important issues, because what affects one partner affects the other as well.

In healthy relationships, both people care about the other's dreams and goals and help and support each other to fulfill them. In this way, they contribute to the happiness of the other and their lives together. It will be a tug-of-war marriage if a spouse strives just to get his or her needs met without caring about the other one's needs. The opposite is much healthier for the relationship. It takes a more mature attitude, a less selfish approach, and love. It has to be mutual caring for each other's well-being. We are in the marriage to give to our spouse what God meant for us to give to him or her. If both people care about the other one's needs being met, they will have a much healthier relationship overall.

If you are not yet married and are interested in finding a mate, ask the Lord to direct you and show you whom He wants to be your husband or wife. He knows so much better than we do what we need.

Selfishness is very childish. We need to grow up and start caring about others. It brings a lot more contentment than striving to get our needs met first all the time. This is true in all relationships. If one person is in it just for what he or she can get and does not care about the other person, it is not a very healthy relationship. This is true for parent and children relationships, friendships, and even business relationships.

We need to ask God for wisdom in choosing friends and whom we do business with. Unholy alliances can cause a lot of grief. Ungodly relationships are very treacherous. We need to ask God to direct us in every area of relationships so that we will have genuine relationships with mutual love, honesty, and respect. This way the relationships are balanced and there is always mutual giving and receiving involved. It means putting others needs ahead of our own at times, but it has to work the other way around as well. Healthy relationships have healthy boundaries.

Friendship

Do not be deceived: "Evil company corrupts good habits" (1 Corinthians 15:33).

And the Scripture was fulfilled which says, "Abraham believed God, and it was accounted to him for righteousness." And he was called the friend of God (James 2:23).

Jesus said:

"This is My commandment, that you love one another as I have loved you. Greater love has no one than this, than to lay down one's life for his friends. You are My friends if you do whatever I command you. No longer do I call you servants, for a servant does not know what his master is doing; but I have called you friends, for all things that I heard from My Father I have made known to you" (John 15:12–15).

Jesus is the greatest Friend of all friends. He is always faithful, always true, always loyal. He never betrays anyone. He is the perfect Friend as well as our savior and redeemer. He can be trusted completely. He will never fail us, and even when we fail Him, He abides faithful!

Jesus was the friend of sinners too. He ate in their homes, visited with them, and went where they were. However, it was not for partaking of what they were doing; it was for influencing them to bring them to the knowledge of the truth. He said we are His friends if we do whatever He tells us. Clearly, Jesus influenced them. It was not the other way around. We need to remember that as well.

The people we associate with will influence us. That is why whom we choose as friends is important. If we compromise our beliefs in order to have friends, it will affect our character. Our closest friends whom we fellowship with should be people of good character.

It is one thing to befriend someone in order to show him or her God's love so he or she will be convinced that God is real and that God is good by our godly example. However, we must not let them influence us so that we are not living the way God's Word says we should. The righteous-living person has to be the example and, thereby, the influence. We must not compromise our standards to get approval from people. We too need to love our neighbors and love those who do not know Jesus so that we will be *"the salt of the earth"* (Matthew 5:13) and *"the light of the world"* (Matthew 5:14). Salt flavors, preserves, and purifies, and light makes the darkness manifest. With the Holy Spirit living in us and the character of Christ, the fruit of the Spirit, growing in us, we are to shine as lights in the dark world around us. We are *in* the world but not *of* the world. We need to bring godly influence to those in the world around us.

God saw that we need each other. He saw that Adam was lonely and needed a mate. We also need friends, and God knows that better than we do. We need to choose them carefully, especially when they are going to influence us.

We need to be true friends who are loyal and honest and uncompromising so that we can be a good influence on our friends. We need to let them be who God made them to be and not try to make them like us or try to manipulate or control them.

Healthy friendships are friendships of freedom. We do not invade the other person's space, and we leave room for them to have other friends. If we do that, we are less likely to strain the relationship. We should not obligate our friends in any way but let them make their choices as we make ours. We give each other "space." Mature friends make room for others in their relationships.

I see all my friends and the new people God brings into my life as opportunities to enrich my life by getting to know them, for not only who they are in the flesh but also who they are in Christ, and what I can learn from them because of what God has put within them to teach me.

If we want to have true and loyal friends, we have to be that kind of friend first. If we are that kind of friend to others, we will reap friends who are that way toward us as well.

Repentance

John came baptizing in the wilderness and preaching a baptism of repentance for the remission of sins (Mark 1:4).

John the Baptist said, "*I indeed baptize you with water unto repentance, but He who is coming after me is mightier than I, whose sandals I am not worthy to carry. He will baptize you with the Holy Spirit and fire*" (Matthew 3:11).

John the Baptist preached the message to prepare the way for the Messiah, the Anointed One, who was coming after him. He baptized them in water, which for Christians is a public or outward confession and submission to identify themselves with Christ in His death, burial, and the resurrection. It is death to the old life and rebirth to the resurrected life in Christ Jesus. "*Therefore, if anyone is in Christ, he is a new creation; old things have passed away; behold, all things have become new*" (2 Corinthians 5:17).

"*For godly sorrow produces repentance leading to salvation, not to be regretted; but the sorrow of the world produces death*" (2 Corinthians 7:10). Godly sorrow produces repentance unto salvation and conversion to being a disciple of Jesus Christ. I do believe there is great need in church for repentance at this time.

Second Chronicles 7:13–14 says,

"*When I shut up heaven and there is no rain, or command the locusts to devour the land, or send pestilence among My people, if My people who are called by My name will humble themselves, and pray and seek My face, and turn from their wicked ways, then I will hear from heaven, and will forgive their sin and heal their land."*

It seems the whole nation was paying the price for the sin of doing it their way, not God's way. God spoke to them about what needed to happen for Him to heal the land. Though this is definitely true for a nation, it is also very critical in the Church. It says to humble ourselves before God, and that means we acknowledge our helplessness and our arrogance and pride, confess it to God as sin, and then pray.

Furthermore, the command is to turn away from all evil and seek His face for the answers, and then we will see God's power in our midst. The Church needs to hear what the Spirit of God is saying to the Church in this hour. We can know and claim the promises of God. That will not work until we heed our responsibility, and that is to obey the conditions to receive those promises of God's blessings. God is waiting for us to hear what He wants us to know and to do first.

It is not just praying more; it is hearing what God has to say and then turning away from everything that is disobedience to God's Word, all the things we have done our own way instead of His way. When God spoke that to Solomon after they dedicated the temple, He also told him that after the people did this, He would hear from heaven, forgive their sin, and heal the land. In verse 15 God said, *"Now My eyes will be open and My ears attentive to prayer made in this place."*

Repentance, which is turning away from sin, should be a way of life for us as Christians. We should let God shine His light in our hearts regularly and then we should turn away from any darkness that shows up in us. Proverbs 20:27 says, *"The spirit of a man is the lamp of the LORD, Searching all the inner depths of his heart."* We need to stay in step with the Holy Spirit and obey the commandments of Jesus. Jesus said in John 14:21, "*He who has My commandments and keeps them, it is he who loves Me. And he who loves Me will be loved by My Father, and I will love him and manifest Myself to him.*"

We cannot ignore the Word of God. Jesus said those who obey the commandments of God are the ones who love Him. How can we say we love God when we disobey His commandments and grieve His Holy Spirit by doing so? That is in direct contrast to the words of Jesus. We as a Church need to get back to the Bible, the simplicity of the gospel of Jesus Christ. The power of God unto salvation is in the message of the cross (1 Corinthians 1:18).

We need to pray as the psalmist in Psalm 139:23–24: "*Search me, O God, and know my heart; Try me, and know my anxieties; And see if there is any wicked way in me, And lead me in the way everlasting.*"

Perseverance

Therefore, having been justified by faith, we have peace with God through our Lord Jesus Christ, through whom also we have access by faith into this grace in which we stand, and rejoice in hope of the glory of God. And not only that, but we also glory in tribulations, knowing that tribulation produces perseverance; and perseverance, character; and character, hope (Romans 5:1–4).

Perseverance means when we are doing the will of God and difficulties, criticism, or opposition comes, we should not quit. We must keep on with all diligence and not lose heart. We have to look to the goal and the results, not the immediate discouragements and obstacles. Galatians 6:9 says, "*And let us not grow weary while doing good, for in due season we shall reap if we do not lose heart.*" We need to keep our sights fixed on the goal.

Persevering means we stay steady and continue despite the difficulties we may encounter along the way. When perseverance is called for, it is usually over a period while we are facing adversity along the path we have to walk. It is not a brief experience but usually a significant period of time in which we have to determine to finish that particular "race." When we know we are doing the right thing in the eyes of God, He will reward us if we do not give up but persevere until we see the victory in the circumstances.

When God puts something in our hearts and opposition or adversity comes, whether it is a result of our own mistakes or persecution from another source, we must keep our eyes fixed on Jesus and persevere in what He would have us do. Second Corinthians 2:14 says, *"Now thanks be to God who always leads us in triumph in Christ, and through us diffuses the fragrance of His knowledge in every place."*

Perseverance means we do not give up. Sometimes along the way we have setbacks we were not expecting, and of course we are then disappointed and discouraged and wonder why it happened. The most important thing is to keep on waiting on God, seeking His face and trusting Him. In the right time, we will reap a harvest for doing what is right in the eyes of God. Perseverance means we persist in doing what we know God wants us to do.

Perseverance means always making the best of the circumstances we are in. Then God sees it and He hears our cry for His help. He is with us, and with His help we can persevere in all things. We must persevere through the things we endure. Hebrews 12:1–2 says,

> *Therefore we also, since we are surrounded by so great a cloud of witnesses, let us lay aside every weight, and the sin which so easily ensnares us, and let us run with endurance the race that is set before us, looking unto Jesus, the author and finisher of our faith, who for the joy that was set before Him endured the cross, despising the shame, and has sat down at the right hand of the throne of God.*

The love of God in our hearts and the faith we have in God give us hope that we will see things we do not yet see. We do not hope for what we can already see. We persevere to see the promises of God fulfilled, because we trust in His Word and His goodness. Romans 8:25 says, *"But if we hope for what we do not see, we eagerly wait for it with perseverance."*

The Blood of Jesus

But Christ came as High Priest of the good things to come, with the greater and more perfect tabernacle not made with hands, that is, not of this creation. Not with the blood of goats and calves, but with His own blood He entered the Most Holy Place once for all, having obtained eternal redemption. For if the blood of bulls and goats and the ashes of a heifer, sprinkling the unclean, sanctifies for the purifying of the flesh, how much more shall the blood of Christ, who through the eternal Spirit offered Himself without spot to God, cleanse your conscience from dead works to serve the living God? And for this reason He is the Mediator of the new covenant, by means of death, for the redemption of the transgressions under the first covenant, that those who are called may receive the promise of the eternal inheritance (Hebrews 9:11–15).

Jesus established the new covenant when He died on the cross. Instead of repeated ceremonial cleansing with the blood of calves and goats, Jesus' sacrifice was made once for the sin of all humanity.

Those Old Testament ceremonial cleansings required the high priest to enter the Most Holy Place of the temple annually to offer a sacrifice for himself and for the sins of the people. The sacrifice of His own blood that Jesus offered cleanses the soul. As the Scripture says, it cleanses our conscience from dead works to serve the living God. Then when He rose from the dead, the victory was complete. Now we too have resurrection life in and through Christ's death and His resurrection. That is why we sing hallelujah for the cross!

Now Christ does not dwell in temples made with hands. First Corinthians 3:16 says, "*Do you not know that you are the temple of God and that the Spirit of God dwells in you?*"

We are righteous through the righteousness of Jesus Christ the Messiah, our Savior and our Lord (2 Corinthians 5:21). He is the King of kings and Lord of lords (1 Timothy 6:15). There is salvation in none other than Jesus (Acts 4:12). The Father gave Him the name that is above every name in heaven, earth, and under the earth. Every knee will one day bow and every tongue will confess that Jesus Christ is LORD (Philippians 2:9–10).

If Jesus gave His life on the cross and there shed His blood once for all and it is forever sufficient for all sin, maybe you ask, why then do we plead the blood of Jesus when we pray? The blood will never lose its power. When we talk about the blood and what it means, when we plead the blood of Jesus over our families, our friends, our hearts or our homes, we are appropriating its benefits, and that power of God moves into the situation. There is power in doing that, and it is supernatural.

There is always a very strong sense of the manifest presence of God when people talk about the blood, sing about the blood, or preach about the blood. Whether we talk about it with our families or friends or the preacher proclaims it from the pulpit, there is an unusual powerful presence of the Lord that becomes evident. Without it there would be no salvation, no eternal life, or hope for any of us.

Forever and ever, the blood of Jesus will never lose its power.

Section 2

My Journey through the Valleys

One night I lay on my bed and contemplated the journey of this life and wondered about many things that have happened to me. I wondered how many of the negative things I have experienced were my own fault and what I should have and could have done different to make life better and happier. I always wonder about things and search for the answers and often come away with more questions instead of a satisfying answer.

I wish I had all the answers in black and white from God, but it just seems some things are never that clear. I have to go on in faith and trust that God is working in my life and that He is happy with what He is doing in my life, even though I am often very dissatisfied with myself and what I have accomplished or the lack thereof. It keeps me searching and seeking His face.

That night was February 13, 2008, and I saw myself standing on the peak of a very tall and very steep snow-covered mountain. I could see to the other side of it now. The mountain I was standing on, the valleys behind me, and everything I saw was under the stark white snow. I looked behind me. Down through the valleys, including the fields, and as far as I could see in every direction, the snow covered everything. All the trees were clothed with hoarfrost. It represented the hardships and the obstacles I had to overcome with God as my Helper and Friend.

It was as though life had been one long, cold, harsh winter!

In the vision even, the slope of the mountain, which I could now see in front of me, was snow-covered right to where it reached the valley on the other side. In the distance, next to the bottom of the mountain where the valley joined to it, was a golden rich harvest field such as I have never seen. I was standing at the very peak of this mountain and looking at the harvest at the bottom of this mountain. Next to the mountain, a valley that was not quite visible still separated me from the harvest field in the distance. I think God was showing me where He wanted to take me. At last, I was at the top of that mountain so that I could see the other side.

As I wrote the first section of this book, I wondered how the part about my own journey was to fit in with the writings the Lord gave me at the time. As I pondered, I seemed to get the understanding that it would be devotional-like but not a January-to-December book as we most often see them, with 365 writings in it. Yet before I started this, it seemed the understanding I was receiving from the Lord was that it would be about my life as well.

How could a devotional book include the journey of my life? I just wrote as the Holy Spirit inspired me, and He gave me the writings one at a time. I did not have an outline in advance. As I obeyed, I wondered how many writings there would be, and it seemed the Lord said there would be fifty. Moreover, at exactly fifty, the inspiration stopped, and I knew that section was complete.

Then He gave me the title for the second part of the book, and as you see, it is about my journey through the valleys. It was in the valleys that the Good Shepherd taught me the things I wrote about in the first part of this book.

I trust Him daily to inspire me as I share the things with you, the readers, that God wants me to tell you. Much in my life has been complicated and convoluted, making it difficult to bring it across to others the way it really was, but I will let God inspire me as I pursue this journey of exposing my valleys to you.

I grew up in a family where there were nine children, seven girls and two boys. I was the second oldest. One brother is older, and the other brother was three years younger than me. He died at age thirty-five of leukemia. Then there were six girls after that. We were an immigrant family to Canada. We were Mennonites, and we moved to Canada from Mexico in the fifties. It was not always a pleasant experience.

Starting in a new school as foreigners, not knowing the language, not having the clothes to dress as the other children did, and coming from a family living in poverty brought some huge emotional problems and baggage with it. I felt very alone, even in a crowd. I longed for love and acceptance, as every human being does, but experienced mockery and rejection because I was different from the others in external ways.

God created us in His image, and we all need others to love and accept us. We also need to be able to give love, have friends, and experience acceptance and affirmation, regardless of our race, nationality, culture, or customs. At the core of our being, we all have the same needs.

My father had very few skills with which to make a living in a new country. Though my parents did the best they could with what they knew, and they too lived with many hardships, many of our needs as children went unnoticed and unmet. Being an immigrant family was not an easy adjustment for any of us. Growing up in that kind of environment does not build emotionally secure children.

My father was a very frustrated person and out of his frustration took many things out on his family. My mother too was a victim of many hardships. There was a lot of verbal abuse in our home. I also remember the whippings I got from my father with his belt. It makes me shudder yet! When now as an adult I reflect on the way it was, I believe my father was a victim of the things he suffered and he had a lot of pent-up anger. The anger very likely was a consequence of deep hurt he experienced in the home he grew up in. Anger that is not dealt with expresses itself in inappropriate ways, and often those not responsible bear the brunt of it.

I did not grow up with the assurance that either of my parents loved me. I do not recall ever hearing those words from either one of them. My mother also was very abusive to me verbally. It seemed she thought of me as her house cleaner and childcare giver for the younger siblings instead of her daughter. I remember times when she told me it was just as much my responsibility to care for and raise my younger siblings as it was hers. I remember her saying these things to me from the time I was maybe ten years old. It did not seem very fair to me, but I could not say anything or defend myself. I felt as though I were a slave to her. She got very angry if I talked back to her, and she often hit me and called me names.

Words of affirmation and encouragement were non-existent during my childhood and teen years as far as I remember. I so needed approval from my mother, but it seemed I never had it. My conclusion was that she hated me, and I never could figure out why. I only wanted her to love me, but it seemed she resented me, because she depended on me and demanded so much of me when I was very young.

I had a huge root of rejection from my mother. It was not until my adult life many years later that the Lord exposed that root in my life and started to heal me of the problems it had caused me throughout life. The root was strong. I felt so unlovable that I could not believe anyone would or ever could love me for who I was, and so I did not like myself. I thought I was ugly and unwanted and unworthy of proper treatment. In retrospect, I know I had no idea what that even looked like or felt like. A root of rejection often pushes others away from us instead of toward us. I rejected myself, and that caused me to believe that everyone else would reject me as well.

Looking back now, I often wonder how much of what I experienced as rejection was perceived rejection instead of actual rejection. Nevertheless, I felt all the pain of it. While I saw others as accepted and loved, it seemed what they had automatically was something I had to earn. I tried hard to be the person I thought I should be and do what I thought I should so that people would accept me. From the time I was a child, there was always an ache in my heart. My heart ached for love and affirmation, which I did not even know how to express. I did all I could for others because I had a lot of love to give, and I know that now. Strangely, it didn't fill the void in my own heart.

Regardless of how I tried to please my parents and even my siblings, it seemed I never could. In school, I always reached out to those who seemed to need friends and those bullied by others. I cared very much, but it seemed no one cared about me. I remember one time when I was maybe nine years old, I brought a book about an orphan home from school. That evening after I had done the work my mother expected me to help with every night, I snuck into a place where I could be alone and read my book. It seemed as though the orphan was the first person I could empathize with. I felt close to this girl while I read the book because as an orphan someone adopted her but in that family she did not feel loved either. She felt all alone, and so did I. I longed for love and acceptance, as every human being does.

I never saw any role models of what it meant for a man to treat a woman the way God would want him to. I had no idea of what a proper relationship would look like with a spouse or even how a man should treat a woman on a date. My parents never told me anything about any of that. The truth is, they probably did not know either. None of us can pass on to our children what we do not have. My parents could not teach us and show us what they did not know, what they did not understand, and what they did not have.

The negative things parents model to their children are generational curses. This goes on until someone along the way recognizes it and chooses to break the link in the chain of the generational curses, finds out the truth, changes the behavior, and models that to his or her descendants. That is how we reverse it and it becomes a generational blessing. We break generational curses by changing our own behavior so we do not pass those negative things on to our children.

At age nineteen, I married a man several years older than I am. He was very domineering. He seemed to want me but had no idea of what marriage really meant. When he asked me to marry him, it never occurred to me that there should be some discussions about his expectations and understanding of the marriage relationship. It just seemed someone actually wanted me and I had better say yes, because likely there would never be anyone else who wanted me.

I used to dream of having a nice little house and being married to someone who loved me and loving him. We would live happily together and love our children in a way that I had never experienced. I expected that shortly before our wedding date the two of us would start looking for an apartment so we could start to set up our own home. One night when my husband-to-be came to pick me up he informed me that he rented a house and he would take me to see it. He told me his mother was there at the time painting the cupboards because they were in very bad shape. He did not discuss it with me; he just did it and then told me—that was the way life went for me from then on.

At that point, I should have recognized the warning signs and put on the brakes. I felt as though something was terribly wrong but could not express what it was. I had no idea why I felt the way I did. It was as though I froze and did not know how to respond.

He had rented an old shack someone had moved into town from a farm. The only room in the house that had running water was the bathroom, and so I had to get all the water from there to do dishes, cleaning, and everything else.

The week after the honeymoon, he informed me of the things he was now going to do, not with me but on his own. He was now joining a bowling league, and he was going to have certain nights out with the boys, and on and on it went. He told me we would have a child right away. It felt as though I had no choice about anything in any way. I did not know how to stand up to him at all.

I found out after we were married that he was in debt. Though he had no sense of proper financial management, he controlled every penny we both earned. When I came home from work on a payday, I had to hand him my paycheck, and I never saw it again. He opened a bank account in his name only, and I had no access to it ever.

I had no idea that I should have some choices and voice them. It felt as though I was drowning or going into shock. He told me how it was going to be, and he never consulted me about anything. I had no boundaries in my life and did not know how to handle it when things frightened me. I did not know how to stand up for myself in anything.

He continued to bully me and intimidate me. I now wonder how anyone could be so terribly naive, but I was. I had no sense of what was acceptable and what was not. He always told me that if any of it bothered me I had a problem—there was nothing wrong with what he was doing. I thought I had to find ways to handle it so that it did not bother me.

A part of me knew something was terribly wrong, even though he convinced me that anything that was wrong was with me. All I knew was, it hurt, and it hurt a lot. I felt very ashamed, and I internalized all the pain and never spoke of it to anyone. A deep sadness came into my heart. I felt very, very lonely.

We got married on December 10, 1966. Early in the new year we had company, and in a crowd my husband joked that he married me for a tax write-off. They all had a good laugh at my expense. I felt worthless and hurt and rejected. After they left I asked him why he said that, and he informed me that he said it because it was true. He laughed again!

Shortly after we were married, a girlfriend of mine wanted to come and spend a weekend with us. When I mentioned it to my husband, he told me that she just wanted to come and see him, because he was so handsome, all the women were after him. He told me she really did not care about me at all; she was just after him. I felt very confused and very insecure and bewildered. I could hardly believe the things I was hearing. It felt like a bad dream.

Those things did frighten me, but he would quickly inform me that if it bothered me it was because I had a problem. I was so insecure that I took that upon myself. If I said anything, he intimidated me and threatened to go to the bar with his friends if I said anything more. That always terrified me because then I would have no idea what was going on. He controlled me completely with fear and intimidation.

Immediately after we were married, he began to flirt with other women in my presence. With that happening all the time, I was afraid he would cheat on me when he went out by himself. That added yet another fear and insecurity to my pitiful life.

Furthermore, my husband told me one time that he never loved me. He just wanted a wife as an anchor to keep him from destroying himself with the lifestyle he was living. He drank a lot at the time. He told me later on that the reason he wanted a child immediately was so it would be harder for me to leave.

Within the first year of our marriage, we had our beautiful daughter. This meant I was at home, and I never had any money, transportation, or any say or control over anything in our house. I did not go back to work, so I had very little interaction with other adults. I was home alone with the baby during the days and often at nights; my husband was out bowling or in the bar. The loneliness was almost unbearable, and I became depressed. It was not a good scene. I longed for security, safety, and stability. There was none of it. I longed for love and felt none in the marriage whatever.

I desperately wanted a good home, a loving home, for our daughter to grow up in. I wanted her to grow up in a secure and loving environment so she would not have all the fears and insecurities that I had. I wanted to give her everything I never had. In my brokenness I did everything I could to be a good wife and a good mother, but the situation quickly took a toll on my emotional and mental health. I suffered a lot in silence, with no one to talk to, ever. No one seemed to notice, and who would care anyway?

I felt as though I were a prisoner instead of a wife. Moreover, I was living in a mental prison. I had issues that seemed to be too big to resolve. It never occurred to me that maybe I should leave. I just wished and daydreamed about a miracle that would take away my pain and my loneliness. That was the only way to survive.

Though I had asked Jesus into my life when I was a child at vacation Bible school, I did not know how to pray or have a relationship with Him. I felt as though I had lost my way. There was never any reinforcement at home from my parents or from anywhere else. I just hoped that Jesus had come when I asked Him to, but I was not sure. I believed there was a good chance He did not want me because I was not acceptable in His eyes either. I felt hopeless, and everything around me seemed sad. I used to laugh a lot, but now my laughter was gone. It felt as though my life had stopped, and now I merely existed without a purpose or any joy. There was nothing to look forward to anymore.

I felt very bad about myself because I could not handle life better, and therefore I thought surely God must be angry with me too. It seemed if I opened my mouth to talk to Him, He was waiting there to hit me over the head with a hammer. Therefore, I did not open my mouth to talk to Him. I was too afraid of Him too. For some reason I saw Him as someone who was just waiting to punish me. It seemed I could never please anyone else, and I was not worthy of love, and even though I longed to please God, it was impossible for me. I saw Him as someone all-powerful who was waiting to get even with me.

I was so troubled I eventually ended up in the hospital in the psychiatric ward. I remember very little about my hospital stay because I was on sedatives and antidepressants. I remember my husband telling me that my doctor told him I needed to talk to a minister, not to them. I have no memory of what I told the doctor, but that was his conclusion.

When I did talk to a pastor who came to see me, he told me that he really felt that I should pray. I could not understand how the man could even think such a thing. I did not know how to pray. I had invited Jesus into my heart many times, but I had no idea how to pray or talk to God at all! It seemed unthinkable to me. However, this man sat with his eyes closed and waited for me to pray. I had told him more than once that my name is Christine, but he always called me "Catherine" for some reason. To this day, I cannot remember what I prayed, but after I did he said, "Catherine, I could feel in my heart when you prayed that you are very close to God."

I was puzzled. I just did not know how he could possibly think that, because I sure did not feel close to God. How could I be? Look at my life! I felt bad all the time and that everything was my fault. If I could be a better person and handle life better I could maybe find some acceptance with God, but certainly not while I felt so depressed. My heart ached all the time, and I seldom laughed anymore. I thought if I could only be the person God wanted me to be, then I would not feel bad about the way things were in my life. My husband had convinced me that things bothered me because there was something wrong with me, and I lived as though it were true. I actually believed it.

I had married a man who was not a Christian and had no interest in the things of God. Although I longed for God and occasionally had the courage to mention that to my husband, nothing seemed to change…until July of 1976, when I had a glorious experience with God and finally had hope again.

The first profound change I remember was an intense desire to pray. It was as though God loosed my tongue, and prayer flowed like a river from my life.

My daughter and I started to go to church with my sister, who had been attending a Pentecostal church for a while. Shortly after that, I was water baptized. The night of my water baptism, as I came up from the water, I started to speak in tongues, but I just had a few words. One of them was *Abba*.

After a few days, as I sat in my usual spot in the living room while I prayed, I sensed or felt someone touch my knees and elbows, and it was as though I was totally at ease and relaxed for the first time in many years. Though I did not see Him, I knew Jesus had come to me. Then my prayers in English turned into a heavenly prayer language, and it flowed like a river. For a couple of weeks it felt as though I could hardly speak in English because of how God released that prayer language in my life. It was another amazing encounter with God, and I will treasure it forever.

My nine-year-old daughter and I went to church regularly from then on, and for the first time in all those years, I had some joy. She told me she wanted Jesus to come into her heart as well. I prayed with her, and she received him as her Savior as well. She received the baptism of the Holy Spirit and had a very strong commitment to the Lord from then on. It was wonderful.

I prayed a lot for my husband, and though he was very resistant to the gospel and coming to church, he eventually did. He too made a commitment to the Lord, but it seemed everything was always more of a struggle for him. Some things changed, but many things did not change in his life. The control and mental and emotional abuse continued.

There was a lot of teaching in the church about wives submitting to husbands and very little if anything ever said about husbands needing to love their wives. He never seemed to be able to overcome his desire and lust for other women, and eventually I could not handle it anymore. I became physically sick. It seemed the emotional pain and the mental torment eventually showed up in my body in the form of physical pain.

Eventually a specialist diagnosed me with a very painful condition called trigeminal neuralgia, for which there is no cure. The only thing doctors could offer were some chronic pain medications, which control it to an extent. I always have pain, but the severity varies. Sometimes it seems as though it is actually getting better. Then something triggers it and it comes back with intensity.

Until someone finally diagnosed it, which took about ten years, no one could explain my pain. I looked fine on the outside but felt as though I were dying on the inside. It became very hard to cope, but I had to make the best of it. I desperately tried to keep doing everything I needed to do. Sometimes the pain was so bad that the fear of living with the pain seemed much worse than death. For years I expected and waited for the Lord to heal me, but that did not happen either.

I continued to seek the Lord and I did not give up. I wanted the Lord to do the work He needed to in me because I still believed that if I could only be fully the person God wanted me to be, everything else would be fine. Nevertheless, the saga continued.

Nothing seemed to change, and eventually God exposed some things that my husband was doing. It devastated me once again. When I finally found out about these things, I prayed harder and harder, but it just seemed I could not pray through for those things. I encouraged him to get help and go for counseling, but he was very resistant to that as well. He did finally talk to a pastor, but it seemed the help he needed was not there. He was not willing to go anywhere else, such as to a counselor, at that time.

Therefore, I just continued to pray and tried to work things out between us, but it just seemed the problem was way beyond what we could handle on our own. The Lord began to speak to me about leaving, and I thought it was the devil. I did not think God would ever say that. I rebuked that voice, and I continued to try and to pray for God's answer to all of this. However, it seemed that voice did not go away. It took me a long time to realize that it was God's voice and that He did want me out of there. Perhaps it would be temporary. At least that is what I hoped. I had a deep love for my husband, and I had always had, it seemed, regardless of how he treated me. I could not imagine life without him.

It terrified me, because I did not have any money or any place to go, and my health was so poor at the time that I did not know how I could possibly get a job to take care of myself. I stayed there for quite a while. I fasted, prayed, and waited for God to say something else, but He did not.

I eventually confided in my own doctor and then one of my friends. My friend said, "You have to get out of there. You cannot stay any longer." I was very frightened by this ordeal. By this time we had been married for over thirty-four years, and I knew no other life. I never even dreamed that it would turn out this way. Through all the years of heartache, it never occurred to me that God would not bring about blessings eventually and that everything would be fine. I never dreamed that God would give this kind of answer. After all, He hates divorce (Malachi 2:16). I knew that, and I hated it too.

I wanted a strong and lasting marriage and a loving home and family. I was far from perfect, but I can honestly say that from the day we were married I put my heart and soul into trying to build a strong and loving marriage and family. Now it was ending like this. It was a valley I never dreamed I would enter, but now it seemed I had to face what God was saying.

The friend I confided in told me I should come and live with her. That was not what I wanted. I did not want to be a burden to someone else. I wanted to take care of myself and not impose on anyone else. Therefore I continued to pray and ask God to provide me with a job so that I could provide for myself. We did not have much as far as earthly possessions were concerned, and I did not feel as though anything we did have was mine or that I would be entitled to something.

The pressure at our house intensified, and I wished that God would just take me home to heaven. I did not know how to take the next step, and I had no confidence to make decisions. One day as I was praying in desperation, the phone rang, and it was that friend of mine. She told me the Lord had spoken to her and told her to phone me one more time and offer me a place to go when I left. Though I knew this was God's answer now, I dreaded it. It still terrified me; I so wished that I could be by myself when I was going through this terrible grief. However, it was God's provision for the time.

That afternoon I packed some clothes, and that evening after supper I left to go to that friend's place. It was definitely a night that I wish I could forget. I longed for bedtime when I could cry by myself, and when it came, I cried until my sides ached. That was a Friday night, and that weekend without my husband was almost unbearable. I longed for him, and I missed him, because I loved him and needed him.

On Sunday morning, I went to church. My pain was so great that I thought I would never feel whole or normal again. That afternoon, I went for a drive through town so that I could cry without anyone seeing me. It was raining, and the rain pelted on the windshield of my car as tears like a river flowed from my eyes. I could not stop crying. The excruciating pain in my heart stayed, and nothing could soothe it even a little bit. I just did not know how I would survive this devastating crisis in my life. I felt helpless, as though I were a bird thrown out on the ocean and I had broken wings so that I could not fly. I was so ashamed and humiliated by the whole experience that I wished I could just hide somewhere. However, I had no place to hide. I had to go back to my friend's house.

She said I could stay there as long as I needed to, but she was going on a trip in a few weeks. It did not seem right for me to be there when she was away. The Lord provided another place for me to stay. There I rented a bedroom and could use the kitchen, but it too was extremely uncomfortable. I felt as though I did not belong anywhere.

I was there for a few months and eventually moved into a basement suite. When I moved there, I thought that surely the Lord did not want me to unpack my belongings. I had no private entrance and very little privacy, and I was used to running my own house. It just did not seem that I could actually live there. I lived there for nearly three years.

One night when the owners of the house, who lived upstairs, were away, some thieves broke in and robbed me as well as the people upstairs. I have not forgotten the creepy feeling I had when I walked into my place. I went downstairs, and it felt as though there were chills going up and down my spine. By this time, I had a part-time job, and though I really liked it, I was very tired sometimes when I got home. That night I had been out for supper, and I was exhausted and looked forward to falling into my bed.

I went to check my voice mail and then noticed that my telephone was gone. They even took the cord. They stole all my good jewelry, some of my electronics, and all of my non-perishable food and my frozen food. They ransacked my bedroom and went through all my personal things. Some of the things they stole were precious to me because they had been gifts that I treasured.

The police officers who came to the crime scene said the thieves very likely planned it and must have known the routine at that house. They told me that part of the city was a bad area for those kinds of crimes. The owners usually parked their camper on the street in front of the house for a couple of days before they left while they were packing everything and getting ready to leave. The thieves would have seen that, and they must have known my routine as well. I usually came home after work, then went out for supper, and returned home shortly after nine o'clock at night.

It was an awful experience. It was sorrow added to sorrow. I did not have tenant insurance, and the property owner's insurance did not cover anything that belonged to me. However, the sense of not being safe and being violated was a much greater loss than the personal possessions the thieves stole. It was a nightmare experience, and I never felt safe there again.

By this time, my husband and I had been living separately for over three years. During that time we always had contact, and I constantly waited on the Lord to see if He would approve us getting back together. Earlier during our separation, my husband did go for counseling for a short time, but then he said he was not going to go for a while but would go back eventually. Up to this time, he had not followed through with it. Moreover, as far as some of the things that separated us, there was very little progress in his life.

I knew I could not stay in that basement suite anymore because I had no sense of safety there at all. I prayed desperately for God to make a way where there seemed to be no way. My husband too was in an apartment, and we discussed the situation. This was very difficult for both of us. That was not the way we were used to living, and neither one of us liked it.

I looked at other apartments but had no peace from God to make a new rental agreement anywhere. One day my husband told me he had looked at some condominiums and would like to buy one so that we could live there together. I did agree to go look, but I did not want to make a decision based on "a nicer place to live." I wanted the will of God for us at the time. There had been so much heartache in our relationship, and I did not want to make an emotional decision that would only lead to more heartache and trouble again.

To make a longer story shorter, we did go look at the condominiums. While we were in one of them, it seemed the Holy Spirit gave me peace about it. It seemed it was fine for me to make this decision now. He did not say I had to do that but He said I now could go back if I wanted to do that.

I made the choice to do that for many reasons. It put our family back together. As lonely as it was, I was determined to be by myself if my husband and I could never get back together. I had no desire to have a relationship with someone else. I took my vows seriously when we got married, and I had no desire for anyone else. To me that was very important, and I was willing to try it one more time.

When Christmas or Easter came, we both spent it with our daughter and her husband and our grandchildren. That was a big reason to give it another chance. Even though our daughter was over thirty years old and married when this happened to us, it still hurt her deeply. For that, I am deeply sorry and have great regrets. I do not know how I could have changed that, but all we can do is let God work in us and bring something good out of the ashes.

Sometime before we got back together I talked to the counselor whom my husband had seen for a brief time. I asked him if he thought it was a good idea for us to get back together. He said no, he could not recommend it, because he did not see what he needed to for him to consider that safe. There would need to be a commitment to long-term counseling on my husband's part first in order to deal with some of the huge issues still very evident. One of those was his unwillingness to communicate openly and honestly. The counselor said otherwise it would be better for a short time and then he would start to do the same things again.

When my husband and I talked about getting back together, I agreed to do it on one condition, and that was that he would go for the needed counseling and stay there until the counselor felt he was ready to stop. He agreed to do that and said he would start after we got back together. He said at the time we had too much to do, such as moving and things pertaining to purchasing a home. Therefore it would be easier to start the counseling once we had moved and felt more settled. So I agreed to that.

I wish I could tell you that it happened and we lived happily ever after, but after we were back together, he acted as though he had never said it. When I started to see the same old patterns surfacing again, I finally, about six months later, reminded him of what he had promised when we agreed to give our marriage another chance. He just said, "Well, I considered it at the time, but I have changed my mind." That part happened exactly as the counselor predicted it would. It broke my heart, but I knew that when he made up his mind, it was settled and the topic not open for discussion. We have never discussed that again.

Some things did change, and he treats me much better in some ways than he ever did before. I try to make the very best of the things that I cannot change and leave those things with the Lord. I do not always succeed, but it is my desire, and I really try. God sees all things, and I want Him to finish the work He has begun in me as well. That is a life-long process, but we need to cooperate with the Holy Spirit in it.

I never stopped loving my husband, and I do not regret the decision we made to give our marriage another chance. Though it is far from perfect, it is a lot better than it used to be. At this time, my husband does not go to church at all. So in that way, I feel like a widow in church. Yet I have the responsibilities of having a husband at home, and I know how important it is to make adequate time and show consideration for him in other ways since he is not involved in anything I am a part of in church. Relationships take thought, planning, and consideration for the needs of the other person. Good relationships do not just happen; we have to plan them and cultivate them.

For us, it takes effort to find things we can do together. At times, it feels lonely, but marriage is a covenant, and we need to take it seriously. A broken marriage seldom hurts only the two people involved. It affects relationships with children and extended family and hurts many people in many cases.

My husband and I have now been back together for nearly four years. I still struggle with rejection at times, but God has done a lot of healing in my life. During the time of our separation, many of these things surfaced, and a lot of healing came into my soul. Though I wish it never happened, and I still struggle with a lot of remorse over the way life has gone, I turn to God daily and ask His help to change the way I think so that it will be more like the way

He thinks. Regardless what life has brought into our paths on this earth—and it is a fact that we are products of what environment we lived in—we have to take responsibility for where we are now.

During those difficult times as a child, I processed things through the eyes of a child. I did not understand that it was not good and it was not what God wanted for me. I learned to cope by withdrawing from others to shield myself from rejection. It seemed to me that if anything good ever came into my life it surely would not last. It would soon be gone again. If anyone ever complimented me, it shocked me. I did not think they really meant what they said. How could anyone see any good in me? It even frightened me. I just wanted to do right and do my best so that I could prove to myself that I could do some things. I did not want anyone to draw attention to those things, because it seemed I would end up not being able to live up to their expectations and they would be disappointed in me. I needed to protect myself from disappointing others because in the end I was convinced I could never please anyone. But I kept trying.

When I look back now, I know that when Jesus came into my life and I finally had the revelation that He accepted me and I had eternal life in Him, I still felt as though I had to be very careful not to do anything wrong, because I wanted His approval desperately. It was a wonderful experience and great relief and peace to have a Friend with whom I could share everything. I cultivated that relationship every day from then until now. I still think that is wonderful.

Though it may sound negative in a way, I also know that the healthy side of that was a reverent fear of the Lord. For that, I am grateful. I did not want to take sin lightly, and I wanted God to work in me to rid my soul of all the dross that remained after I was born again of God's Spirit. My mind, of course, needed renewal by God's Word.

At first, I experienced joy that was like a taste of heaven. I experienced love that was straight from heaven. I felt safe and secure for the first time in my life. I felt anchored and as though a strength had come into me that was not my own. I longed to know God intimately, and I felt a very strong call to prayer and many times fasting as well.

It was not long afterwards that the winds of adversity came and my faith was severely tested. There were valleys so painful that it seemed I would not survive. Some of them were things God was doing and other things the enemy was using. Either way, how we respond determines who we will become. The challenges of growing up spiritually came in many different ways, and often the tactics of the enemy were very subtle. I asked the Lord for a wise and discerning heart so that I would know what He was saying and not just listen to all the other voices around me.

Regardless of what happened or how painful it was, I always turned to God first and stayed in touch with Him. He was my only help and refuge, and I knew that. The dreams the Lord gave me that I wrote about in my first book, *Keep It Simple, Saints*, were very real in my heart, and I knew God had plans for my life that were beyond what I understood.

One of the things He was preparing me for was to write. I had a very vivid dream that foreshadowed it, but at the time I had no idea what it meant. I just knew that God had spoken to me in that dream. It took me a long time to understand that He was speaking to me about writing.

In another vivid dream, I was standing on a podium and speaking into a microphone. I was wearing a basic dress, which was blue. As the dream progressed, the dress was green, and at the end of the dream the dress was red. As the years went by I came to understand that when the dress was blue I was a citizen of the kingdom of heaven, a Christian. The green dress meant growth in spiritual development and understanding of the Bible, which is God's Word. The red dress meant ripe fruit, or maturity. The basic dress was there, but it did not have the sleeves on it yet, and I did not have the shoes to go with it. I was waiting on God, and that much I knew.

It seemed the dream meant that God was preparing me for a speaking or preaching ministry. So far I have done very little of that other than in small groups or one-on-one ministry. Occasionally I have done some, but not to the extent that it seemed the dream meant I would be.

I have no formal training, but I have cherished and studied God's Word for many years so that I will have it in my heart and understand it. If I teach others, I want to apply the Word of God rightly, as instructed in 2 Timothy 2:15. I did some courses through correspondence and took every opportunity available to me in the church, such as courses or seminars held there. I read, meditate, and study God's Word regularly, and I have a longing to know Him better every day. Often, when I reflect upon the things that have happened over the last thirty or more years, I realize that though I have an intense longing to know God and understand His Word, the longer I know Him the more I realize how little I know.

The Snow-Covered Mountain

It is now September 23, 2008, and my writing has been on "hold" for some time now. I have not had the freedom to continue since about the middle of June. I thought the book was nearly finished, and then as I was writing one day, the aforementioned dream came to mind and it seemed I should write it down, although I felt reluctant to do so. After I wrote about it, I clearly sensed that it was now time to wait. I found that very challenging, since I thought the book was nearing the completion point and I was eager to get it done.

Although I had no understanding about why I needed to wait, it was clear that I had to wait. I wondered if I was hearing from God and if I was heading in the right direction when I wrote about that dream or if I should delete it and pursue the writing in a different way. I experienced silence. That was agonizing. Why should I just wait? I needed to finish the work I started, and I wanted to see how the Holy Spirit would direct me to finish it.

On Sunday morning, September 21, 2008, while I was sitting in church listening to my pastor's sermon, I finally began to sense the inspiration for what I am writing now. I remembered the vision I had that I wrote about in the opening of "My Journey through the Valleys." I now understood something I did not understand at the time I first saw it.

However, at last, I was standing at the very peak of the mountain and I could see the other side. Yet I knew I had to go down the mountain before I could step into the harvest field. The harvest field was a slight distance from the bottom of the mountain. As I waited, I understood that there was something not visible in between the bottom of the mountain and the harvest field—an indefinable valley. I had no idea what it would involve. I just knew it was there and I could not get to the harvest field until I walked through it. I was somewhat afraid, since I had no idea what would happen next. Would it be pain, sorrow, heartache, or would it be something wonderful to look forward to instead of another struggle or hardship to face? I had no idea, and God was telling me nothing more right then.

My husband had plans to retire at the end of the year, but then suddenly his employer offered him a retirement package effective within one month. That was going to bring some major adjustments into our lives, and we both knew that. Maybe that is why the writing had to wait. This might change what God would do in my life now.

The Indefinable Valley

On September 24, 2008, toward the end of my devotional time with my Lord, as I sat listening I wondered about that valley, and I asked my Lord if He would tell me what was there or what it meant. I knew I was at the peak of that very steep mountain, and I was well aware that I still needed to come down before I could even approach that valley. That mountain was so steep that it was obvious it would be humanly impossible for me to walk down from it. As I looked down and saw that long and sharp descent to the bottom, I wondered how I would ever get down there.

Then I saw the Good Shepherd. He appeared very strong and confident and even amused at what He saw. He was extending His hand to me as though He expected me to take His hand and then jump down. It looked like a huge and even frightening plunge to take and certainly humanly impossible to survive. Yet it seemed that He was waiting for me to trust Him to that extent. I pondered these things, and I had no idea what it would be when it actually happened.

Then He gave me a faint glimpse into the valley that I could not see before. There was what appeared as a stream or river. In that stream was a crossroads or an intersection. To get to the harvest field on the other side I had to make a decision to cross that river. The other way would be to go with the flow of the stream—the natural current.

I wondered what it meant. It seemed if I wanted to get to that harvest field, I would have to go contrary to the flow. I wondered if going with the flow of that stream meant to follow the crowd or the status quo. All I could do is wait expectantly and be attentive to what the Good Shepherd was saying to me.

In that valley, it seemed, I would find the basket. I needed to carry the pearls into the harvest field, where I could distribute them.

The Promise of God

Daily I sought the Lord's face, waiting for direction to continue the writing He had asked me to do. The only time I saw anything clearly was on October 14, 2008. I saw a very colorful rainbow over my head, over the outside door that leads into my home, and over my car. It was a reminder that God will never forget the promises that He gives to His own children. In addition, all we need to do is trust Him and obey; the rest is up to Him. When He says wait, we must wait, and when He says do this or that, we quickly do what we know He is asking. He cannot work with people who will not listen so that they might hear or those who will not do what He asks. He wants us to learn to hear and then be quick to obey. The promises of God keep me whether at home or away, and He is with me wherever I go. He never leaves me alone.

Interlude with God

On October 23, 2008, I left for Comox, British Columbia. My sister and her family live there. It was my annual visit to the coast to be with them and to attend the women's conference at their church. The theme for the conference was "Interlude with God" and the message came across in many different ways—God is waiting for His people to spend time and develop an intimate relationship with Him.

The conference speaker told us that when she was on the plane coming from California and not far from the Comox airport, she was talking to God. She asked Him what He wanted her to tell the women at the conference. The Lord showed her a picture of ants on an anthill. They were looking down, one following the other, doing the same thing repeatedly, and they were busy.

She said the Lord told her that His people are busy, like the ants. However, He is not asking them to be busy; He is asking them to listen to Him so that they can do what He asks, and that is a lot different from just being busy.

It seems that is the cry of God's heart to His people. Meanwhile, they would rather be busy than wait and listen until they hear His instructions and then simply do what He says. The busyness results in weariness and unfruitful efforts a lot of the time, but it seems it is hard for people to return to the lost art of waiting in God's presence.

The Canoes in the River

Daily I continued to wait in God's presence and listen for His voice. On October 29, 2008, I saw the stream in the valley again. There were three canoes at the intersection I saw earlier in the stream or river. One was facing upstream; another was heading downstream. In between the two canoes was a third one, and it was going across the stream. I was standing in that one, and it was very difficult to maintain my balance and keep my focus because the other two kept bumping into the canoe in which I was standing and my focus was to get to the other side. They were a great hindrance to me moving forward.

I believe the two canoes that kept bumping into me represented the opposition that I was facing in my determination in getting to where the Lord wanted me to go. It seemed the other two boats or canoes were keeping me trapped there so that I could not move forward to my destination, which was the other side and then that harvest field.

At this point, I was feeling very unsure of myself. I was asking myself questions such as, Am I really hearing from God? and How long will He have me wait before He allows me to continue the writing of this book so that I can complete it? These can be times of anguish, and they certainly were for me.

The Concrete Wall

On November 11, 2008, to my surprise I saw a huge concrete wall at the edge of the river. I wondered how I could possibly cross that tall concrete wall to step onto the shore and head for that harvest field I knew was in the distance on the other side of the river. It must represent another huge obstacle that I cannot overcome without supernatural intervention from God Himself. *Why does He show me the concrete wall without showing me what it represents or how to get past it?* This question went through my mind and heart daily. Did God want me to do something that would bring that wall down, or was it simply there for His use, so that when His time came, the wall would come down? Did it have anything to do with me? Was it my own fault the obstacle was there? I heard…silence.

The Clear Water

On November 12, 2008, I saw some clear, clean water coming from the drab concrete wall. It was as though it were crystal because it appeared so pure and so clean. It was amazing to me to see water coming from that wall. It was certainly not what I would have expected there.

As I continued to look at it, I saw myself in that water. It was like being in a waterfall. It washed over me and right through me, as though my flesh was no barrier for that cleansing water. I saw myself being clothed in a gown that was a very healthful flesh-colored pink. The water continued to wash over me.

God uses anguish, frustration, grief, uncertainty, and inward struggles to purge our souls and transform us into what He wants us to become. We cry over what is happening to us, while God rejoices over what He is doing in us.

The Hammer of God

Periodically as I focused on that wall, I saw a hammer made of transparent fire. Surely it was the hammer of God's Word. It was pounding away at the concrete wall. Yet there was no evidence of it cracking. How could one hammer shatter that huge concrete wall so that I could cross over to the other side?

On November 19, 2008, I saw that fiery hammer pounding away at the wall again. With one final blow it caused the wall to part, similar to how the Red Sea parted for the Israelites when they were leaving Egypt. All I knew that day was that it parted the wall, and I did not know what would happen next.

The next day, I saw myself move quickly forward as though the Spirit of God carried me swiftly to the other side. Instead of moving forward in that canoe, I was immediately on the other side of the wall. The wall closed behind me, and I could not see anything on the side behind me anymore. The canoes vanished, almost as though they had never been, and I could never even look back there again. The concrete wall closed behind me, and I disappeared out of my sight. I have no idea what it will look like and what is going to happen now. As I see it in the spirit, I write it here for you to read.

Inevitable Changes

Here I wait, and it is now December 1, 2008. The Lord is asking me to write about some of the changes in our household in the last few months.

In late August, my husband informed me that his employer offered him a retirement package. Since he needed to retire anyway in the near future, for health reasons and simply needing to lay down some of the responsibilities, which were becoming a burden at his age, it was too good to reject. So on very short notice, he became officially retired on September 30, 2008.

It was, of course, a huge adjustment for him as well as for me. I was used to having the house to myself during the days from Monday to Friday. Now he is here all the time, and it has certainly brought about some changes in both our lives. These are changes that one can only make when they become inevitable and the choice is no longer one's own.

We found it necessary to make some changes to reduce our monthly budget. One of those changes was to downsize to one vehicle for the two of us. Up until now we each had a car to drive. If one was going in one direction, it did not mean the other one could not go in the other direction. Though I knew we needed to make this change before long, it too came suddenly one day when I was not expecting it.

My husband left the house shortly after noon one Friday to do an errand that would take less than an hour. He did not return for about three hours. I was concerned something might have happened to him since he had not called and I did not know where he could possibly be for that long. When he drove into the driveway, he was not in his car. He came walking toward the door with another man. I thought he must have had an accident. However, it was a car sales representative with him, and they came to take me for a drive in the van that my husband wanted to buy.

The sales representative drove my car to the lot for appraisal, and my husband followed in the van with me beside him. The two of them quickly informed me of all the reasons I should want this van. My initial response was one of utter surprise. I never dreamed of driving a van and was not the least bit excited about it.

My husband wanted to write up a contract to purchase the van immediately. I said, "Can we at least go home and sleep on this?" He said no, because the sales representative was going away and would not be back in the office until the following Monday. My husband was sure that if we did not make a deal that night, someone else would buy the van he wanted. I asked if we could not at least go home and have dinner, since it was ready. That way we could at least talk about it and make a decision with more thought put into it. He said no, it needed to be done right then. Therefore, it was.

The following Tuesday we delivered our cars. We left both cars behind and replaced them with one van. My car represented a piece of my independence. Now it was gone. That night I went to bed and felt as though something was lost. I prayed for the Lord to help me adjust to these changes. I knew that my attitude was very important and that it would affect how simple or difficult these changes would become. Circumstances change and some changes are inevitable. We may not always welcome changes. However, we have to face them, and then God helps us.

These experiences are like chapters of our lives now written, and we cannot take them back. We have to embrace the new chapters of life and choose to see the good in the way it is now instead of clinging to the way it once was. Life moves on. There are times when we mourn the loss of what once was, but time moves on and we can choose how we are going to view it. In everything God helps us if we invite Him into the situation, and He has certainly helped us.

The Christmas Season

As I waited for God to give me some insight and what He wanted me to write next, I kept thinking about that concrete wall. Though it appeared to be an insurmountable obstacle, I seemed to be on the other side. However, there was nothing there. I could not see anything there, as though it was night and it was dark all around me. I did not consciously think that I wanted to go back to where I had been in that struggle, but as I prayed and asked the Lord about it, I saw myself still trying to climb that wall and look behind me. Finally, I got a glimpse of what was back there, but all the things I had seen there before were gone. I could not see the stream or the canoes—not even the snow-covered mountain. There was just a pile of gray ashes.

The obstacle was now behind me, but all I could see in front of me was bleakness. I could not see a pathway in front of me or beside me. What did God want me to do? It was bleak all around me.

One day shortly before we left for Calgary to spend our holidays with our daughter, her husband, and our two grandchildren, in the bleakness around me I saw a Christmas tree. That was all. I could see nothing else.

We had a very nice time with family in Calgary. We attended a beautiful Christmas Eve service in the church they attend. The congregation sang Christmas carols with enthusiasm, and the pastor's warm and meaningful message touched our hearts even though we had all heard the true message of Christmas many times. Christmas Day was delightful—especially watching our little grandchildren open their gifts and seeing the expressions on their little faces.

The weather was frightfully cold, and it was a gorgeous white Christmas. Traveling was somewhat of a challenge. As we drove home, I wondered what this next year would bring and what the Lord would do in our lives. It seems we cannot figure it out in advance. However, we have the promise that God's Word is a lamp to our feet and the light will illumine our path as God sees fit. When He wants us to act, He will let us know. Until then, we wait and sit at His feet. Until He gives further direction, we walk in the light that we already have. The light we already have is the lamp at our feet. It tells us what we need to do today. God will give us a new wick in our lamp for tomorrow. Moreover, He will provide the light we need to obey Him each day.

It is December 30, 2008, and it seemed appropriate that I should write this today. Soon it will be a new year.

The New Year

Today is January 5, 2009. Our New Year's Eve and New Year's Day were very quiet. We did have another turkey dinner with all the trimmings. I pondered the things that have happened, and I wondered what the new year would bring. Life seemed dull and uneventful at this time.

I could see nothing ahead of me. I still longed for purpose and fulfillment, something that would satisfy my longing soul. I longed to see more of what God was doing and to understand how I am to do my part in the remaining time I have in this life. In times such as this, I wonder if my Heavenly Father has anything left for me to do or if I just have to exist from one day to the next. I waited in God's presence to hear something, whatever He had to say or whatever He wanted me to see.

Two days ago, I saw that the Christmas tree was gone, and Jesus was standing where it had been. He looked very pure, dressed in a glistening white robe, and He looked very confident, even though I had no confidence at this point. Other than that, everything looked bleak around me. I saw nothing else at the time.

It appeared as though He might bring some enlightenment soon. Maybe this meant more inspiration, revelation, and direction for the future. I knew one thing, that I was more desperate than ever before. I realized more than ever that without Him, I can do nothing. Without Him, I am helpless, hopeless, and useless on this earth.

Unless His Spirit inspires me, leads me, and empowers me, I am useless. It does not feel good to my flesh. I long for Him, and I long to experience some joy again. It seems so long since I really experienced the joy of the Lord. The Bible says that the joy of the Lord is our strength (Nehemiah 8:10). If joy is our strength, then sorrow is the opposite. I do not feel strong right now, I feel weak. Again, the Bible says in 2 Corinthians 12:9, *"And He said to me, 'My grace is sufficient for you, for My strength is made perfect in weakness.' Therefore most gladly I will rather boast in my infirmities, that the power of Christ may rest upon me."*

When we recognize our human weaknesses and acknowledge them, we position ourselves for God's power, His Spirit, to work in us, through us. We enter into a place where His Spirit can rest upon us. We do not struggle to do it without Him anymore.

Lush Green Foliage

That night I woke up several times and yearned for answers to many needs in the lives of family members, friends, and hurting people I know about. In addition, I desperately longed to hear God's voice about some of the answers I need from Him for my own life.

Early in the morning on January 6, 2009, I awakened again. There in the distance I saw another mountain. I was at the top. Unlike the snow-covered mountain, this one was covered with lush green foliage. It was so dense that I could not see the surface of the mountain at all. Everywhere I could see, this mountain was lush and green with foliage. Even at the bottom of it the grass was very green. It seemed there was nothing to dread anymore, but good things were ahead. It seemed the future was bright.

In the vision or the picture I saw, I was wearing a red dress, and it was complete. The sleeves were on it, and all the final changes were there at last. I was wearing new shoes that looked as though they came from a pearl.

Later on as I spent time with God, I saw a bright light on the inside of me. It affected every part of my being—spirit, soul, mind, and body. I pondered what I saw. I wondered, *Could this mean that hardships are finally over, at least for now, and illumination from God is coming soon?*

Eagles Wings

It is now January 29, 2009. Daily I wait for God's voice to give me direction, inspiration, enlightenment from His Word, and something to comfort me while I wait for the conclusion of this book. It seems something needs to happen before I can complete this writing. Is there something I need to do? Or do I have to wait for God to do something that will bring the conclusion to this? Right now, I am not sure. I listen, expect, and continue to wait.

The deep longings of my heart to experience the fulfillment of what seems to be "unfulfilled" as to the promises I had from God, or thought I did, are like a deep ache in my heart. They even hurt in my bones, it seems. It feels as though something is contained that I should be able to release, and it hurts day and night. Nevertheless, where can I find the answer—unless I wait until my Beloved Savior gives me the answer? Until then I ponder all these things in my heart. Unless the Lord brings it about, it will never happen, for without Him I am nothing and I can do nothing worthwhile.

I see an eagle coming toward me as I sit here in God's presence. He is coming to scoop me upwards, and I am now standing with one foot on each of his wings. We are soaring upwards above the clouds. We are high above the clouds, just gliding along. I look down, because I am anxious to see what it looks like down there from this perspective, and all I can see are those ugly gray ashes.

Though many of us encounter suffering, pain, and hardships of various kinds, in order to embrace any of those things we need to learn to see them from God's perspective. It is not the suffering that brings glory to God but the resurrection that comes after the suffering. He works in us for His good pleasure. His pleasure does not come from our suffering, but those things are so temporal compared with the glory that is to come. He uses those things to transform us into the likeness of His own Son, and that is His purpose for us. Then we can shine like stars in a dark world around us. We are to be the light of the world and the salt of the earth. Light shows up the darkness, and salt purifies, preserves, and adds flavor.

Conclusion

February 10, 2009

The basket that will contain the pearls is this book. The valley I have been walking through has been the valley of bleakness. The time of waiting has not been easy, and I have so many questions all the time. Nothing seems to come as clearly as I would like it to. What does the Lord want me to do and how does He want me to share my experiences with you? Sometimes when I most need to hear from God, or think I do, everything seems cheerless, dreary, and barren. In faith I stay the course. I continue because somewhere God will bring the light and it will all make sense again.

Hindsight is always clearer. It is oftentimes when we look back that we truly see how faithful God has been when it seemed He was not hearkening to the cry of our hearts and His voice did not come. When the time is right and He is ready to move us forward, it becomes very clear that He has been right there with us all the time. Though His presence was not visible and not even felt, His promise is sure that He will never leave us nor forsake us. In these times, we are learning to trust more and more in His Word, and we learn that He is faithful to His Word all the time.

February 14, 2009

Today is Valentine's Day and a special time to think of those we love and honor them in appropriate ways. I remembered the things about my mother that made her special to me. I thought of the things she used to bake—the world's greatest cinnamon buns, her wonderful dinner rolls, and her fabulous chocolate pie. In my heart I thanked her for those special treats.

It made me reflect and see how unique each person is and how there is something in every person that makes them special to someone. Though she has been with Jesus now for several years, I wish I could go and have some of her treats with a good cup of coffee and just have a visit with her. It is as though I still long to know her approval. I am sure when we meet again, when I also leave this earthly tent, I will have that approval and we will have a great visit. I am not sure if there will be dinner rolls, cinnamon buns, or chocolate pie and coffee, but perhaps there will be.

February 15, 2009

God spoke to Jeremiah and told him that before He had formed Jeremiah in his mother's womb, He knew him, sanctified him, and ordained him to be a prophet to the nations. Jeremiah reminded the Lord that he was still very young and so he did not think he could speak eloquently to the people. However, God told him not to say those things but to go and speak whatever He commanded him. He said to not be afraid of the people or their faces, for God would be with him. Then the Lord touched Jeremiah's mouth and told him that He had put His words in Jeremiah's mouth (Jeremiah 1:1–9).

Just as the Lord knew Jeremiah before his conception in his mother's womb, so God saw us and knew just what our lives would be like on this earth. Our parents, our childhood, and what life brings to us are some of the things that determine who we are and who we will become. Those life experiences combined with the abilities, talents, and spiritual gifts God gives us make us who we are. They include what others have done that hurt us or helped us and the choices we made ourselves, those that were good and those that caused us hurt. We all have our share of self-inflicted wounds caused by our own mistakes. Whether we caused it ourselves or someone else caused it, our pain must be reconciled in our hearts before God. We have to relinquish our pain and our past. Then healing flows into our lives and through us to others.

What we do does not make us who we are. On the contrary, we do what we do because of who we are. What we do is the expression of who God has made us. Out of what God does in us, we bring forth what He pours out through us if we yield to His Spirit.

Some of us may not be proud of the way we grew up or what our heritage is, but rather than resent those things, we must learn to embrace them. When we embrace our pain and face it, we can ask God to redeem it and use it for His glory. When we do that, we bring to others the same message that God gave us when His redemption came into our lives. The very things that hurt us the most are the things that can help others the most when we offer those ashes to God. He can then use us to bring comfort to others who are presently experiencing what we did then. If we let God redeem our pain and use it for the good of others, then we have not wasted anything.

If we surrender all of it to God and let Him use it to help others, He will be with us the same as He was with Jeremiah. He never leaves us without His help when we reach out to others. He is with us, and He will fill our mouths with His words as well.

February 20, 2009

After I reached the other side of that huge concrete wall and wanted to reach back, as though I needed to know or remember what was there or see what was going on there now, I saw only ashes. I saw the wall as a huge obstacle that I could not overcome without supernatural intervention from God. Humanly, it was insurmountable. His Word parted the wall and opened the way for me to move to the other side. Yet I could not see what I needed to do there at the time or even right now. What was very clear is that I cannot go back there; I have to stay on this side of the wall. That is history, and now I have to move on.

We need to deal with things holding us back from pursuing God's call on our lives, so that we can fully focus on what lies ahead. That includes letting go of things we thought or things we expected God to do that have not happened. Our main goal is to know Him more and more all the time. Then we keep our eyes on the ultimate goal, which is to spend eternity with Him and receive the rewards for having obeyed Him.

Learning to know Him also involves suffering at times. It is in those times that we seek Him the most. When we do, He can work in us more effectively to transform us into the likeness and character of His own dear Son, the Lord Jesus Christ. We cannot change anything we have done or anything anyone else has done to us, and letting go of it is a choice, the same as forgiveness is. It may not feel that way at first, but when we follow a right course of action, the right feelings eventually follow the choice we have made. We must stop dwelling on what has gone wrong and choose to trust that God can use us in spite of all those things, even if we are not proud of them.

It does not mean we do not remember things anymore. It just means we do not let them hinder us anymore. We do not waste time thinking about how those things will keep us from doing what we know God wants us to do. This takes active discipline in our thought life. We can learn to control our thoughts. In the Bible we find out what God says is true about those who have received righteousness through Christ's atoning death and resurrection. Those are the thoughts we must dwell on. That is how we change and renew our old defeating thought patterns to thinking the way God's Word instructs us. We must let the Bible transform the way we think.

We must let go of our pasts and all the things that have gone wrong. If we do not, we cannot enjoy the journey and focus on where we are going instead of being bound by where we have been and what we have done wrong in the past. It means living in freedom from our pasts and accepting the righteousness in Christ freely given to us, and that qualifies us for the things God calls us to do.

Romans 12:1–2 says,

> *I beseech you therefore, brethren, by the mercies of God, that you present your bodies a living sacrifice, holy, acceptable to God, which is your reasonable service. And do not be conformed to this world, but be transformed by the renewing of your mind, that you may prove what is that good and acceptable and perfect will of God.*

March 4, 2009

I know that God is speaking to me about letting go of the things I regret and the things I still ponder and wish I could change about past decisions and mistakes, but history is history. What we have done, we have done, and even God cannot change that. We have written those chapters of our lives, and all we can do now is glean wisdom from them in order to pursue what lies ahead and to do it with courage and enjoy the journey.

The best way to learn is from the mistakes of others. To learn from our mistakes is the next best thing. If we do not learn from either one, we are fools.

When I saw that huge concrete wall, I knew that to me it appeared as huge, insurmountable obstacles that were humanly impossible to overcome. No human power can part a concrete wall and open the way for what lies ahead—and then close it behind us. Only God can do that. We have to cooperate with Him in order for that to happen so that we can be happy now and not mope over what has been in the past. Easier said than done, of course—but with God's help it is always possible.

Overcoming is not just "trying harder" or striving to get to places we have not yet been. It is "yielding" to the Spirit and the Word of God. We surrender to the life of God within us so that we are able to live in a place of peace and rest. The victory comes from a position of rest; we have decided to trust in Him, that He will work all things out in His perfect way and His perfect time. We cease from our human efforts and ambition, and we let Him have His way in our lives and in our circumstances.

Our anxieties usually pertain to the physical or material things that concern us. These are the very things Jesus said we are not to fret about because God knows we need them.

Matthew 6:25–34 says,

> "Therefore I say to you, do not worry about your life, what you will eat or what you will drink; nor about your body, what you will put on. Is not life more than food and the body more than clothing? Look at the birds of the air, for they neither sow nor reap nor gather into barns; yet your heavenly Father feeds them. Are you not of more value than they? Which of you by worrying can add one cubit to his stature? "So why do you worry about clothing? Consider the lilies of the field, how they grow: they neither toil nor spin; and yet I say to you that even Solomon in all his glory was not arrayed like one of these. Now if God so clothes the grass of the field, which today is, and tomorrow is thrown into the oven, will He not much more clothe you, O you of little faith? Therefore do not worry, saying, 'What shall we eat?' or 'What shall we drink?' or 'What shall we wear?' For after all these things the Gentiles seek. For your heavenly Father knows that you need all these things. But seek first the kingdom of God and His

righteousness, and all these things shall be added to you. Therefore do not worry about tomorrow, for tomorrow will worry about its own things. Sufficient for the day is its own trouble."

March 10, 2009

The time has come to finish this book. This will be my last entry for the conclusion. This morning during my devotional time, when I least expected it, the Lord spoke to me and said I could close this now. I wondered why, since I did not feel I had anything more to write now than I would have had weeks ago. Though it seemed something needed to happen before I could adequately conclude this and it was important that I waited so that it would be accurate, nothing dramatic or explosive has transpired. I believe I had to pass the waiting test to see if I would wait until the Holy Spirit gave me the "green light" to finish this.

I used to think the only way God could use our voices was to preach, but I think the voice He has given me is coming through my writing. I can do that from my own home and reach as many as will read the book. Even though we may unintentionally miss some of things God calls us to do, He will work things out in His time and in His way.

Have you been through seasons in your life when it seemed God was not listening to your prayers? You needed direction desperately, but it seemed there was none forthcoming? Perhaps we all have been there many times, and when the answer comes, it seems as though it is really no big deal. But during the wait, we pressed in to God, and we grew in our love relationship with Him. In these times, we are learning to listen and to wait for God and willingly be dependent on Him.

I am not saying we will feel comfortable during the wait, but we need to let the Holy Spirit lead us, inspire us, and give us direction all the time. We learn to have Him direct us in our everyday lives so that we are truly living lives ordered by the Lord. It takes discipline to do this. Nonetheless, this is the way we develop our ear to listen and hear His voice so that we can obey Him.

God works in us during these times, and to Him that is the most important thing. His work in us is the transformation to bring about the likeness and character of Christ so that we will reflect Him more perfectly to the world around us.

Philip asked Jesus to show him the Father and it would be sufficient for him. In John 14:9–11 Jesus gave Philip this answer:

> *"Have I been with you so long, and yet you have not known Me, Philip? He who has seen Me has seen the Father; so how can you say, 'Show us the Father'? Do you not believe that I am in the Father, and the Father in Me? The words that I speak to you I do not speak on My own authority; but the Father who dwells in Me does the works. Believe Me that I am in the Father and the Father in Me, or else believe Me for the sake of the works themselves."*

Jesus is in the Father, and the Father is in Him. God dwells in us by His Holy Spirit when we become His children. The fruit of the Spirit, or the nature of God, grows in us as we commit ourselves to His discipleship. That means we are followers of Jesus, and everything we do is under the authority of God's Word and His Holy Spirit. If His Word and Holy Spirit instruct us to do certain things, even if everyone around us is going in the opposite direction, a disciple of Jesus must go God's way. Then we have peace with God and His peace rules in our hearts; we are becoming one with Him more and more all the time. We live in harmony and unity with Him, His Holy Spirit, and His Word. Joshua 1:8 says, *"This Book of the Law shall not depart from your mouth, but you shall meditate in it day and night, that you may observe to do according to all that is written in it. For then you will make your way prosperous, and then you will have good success."*

Your unfulfilled dreams may look differently when God brings them about than the way you pictured it when He first put them in your heart, so keep following the Lord and do not give up. From my perspective, I saw the ashes. From God's perspective, He sees the beauty that He is able to bring forth from the ashes.

First Corinthians 13:11–13 says,

When I was a child, I spoke as a child, I understood as a child, I thought as a child; but when I became a man, I put away childish things. For now we see in a mirror, dimly, but then face to face. Now I know in part, but then I shall know just as I also am known. And now abide faith, hope, love, these three; but the greatest of these is love.

I do not know what God will do next in my life. However, God willing, and if He gives me the inspiration, I will update you on the journey in my next book.

Epilogue

I started this book in November, 2007. The one thing I preferred not to write about was my personal life. It was too full of regrets, heartache, shame, pain, and embarrassment. However, that is what my Heavenly Father wanted me to put into writing. It is my prayer that our loving Heavenly Father will place this book in the hands of others who will receive hope, encouragement, and strength to persevere in their lives as well.

Though there are things others did to us to shape us, such as our childhoods, over which we had no control, we eventually have to take responsibility for our choices. The way out of victim mentality is to take responsibility and break generational curses with changed behavior that is in harmony with God's Word and His will for us. Though in our childhoods parents, teachers, and other children did things to wound us, the solution does not come from blaming them for our problems.

My purpose in sharing these things with you is to point you to the only One, the Good Shepherd, who is able to restore us. With His help and our cooperation and perseverance, we overcome those things and we become victorious rather than victims of our pasts.

As we recognize our total dependence on God, we are able to draw more and more strength from Him. He promises to give us wisdom for life and to do it liberally if we will just come to Him and ask. Faith is very different from presumption. Faith is total dependence on God, and presumption is acting on the assumption that we know what God wants to do.

Jesus said He does only what He sees His Father doing. *"Then Jesus answered and said to them, 'Most assuredly, I say to you, the Son can do nothing of Himself, but what He sees the Father do; for whatever He does, the Son also does in like manner'"* (John 5:19). Jesus told us that He was very dependent on the Father to do the works He did. He told us the Father was in Him, He was in the Father, and they are one. *"I and My Father are one"* (John 10:30). Moreover, in John 10:37–38 Jesus said, *"If I do not do the works of My Father, do not believe Me; but if I do, though you do not believe Me, believe the works, that you may know and believe that the Father is in Me, and I in Him."*

In John 15:1–8 Jesus left us the following words to show us that we too must depend on Him and His words must abide in us or we cannot bear holy fruit. We cannot produce any fruit without Jesus. We need Him in us, God the Holy Spirit working through us, so that we can be one with Jesus and the Father, the same as it is with them.

> *"I am the true vine, and My Father is the vinedresser. Every branch in Me that does not bear fruit He takes away; and every branch that bears fruit He prunes, that it may bear more fruit. You are already clean because of the word which I have spoken to you. Abide in Me, and I in you. As the branch cannot bear fruit of itself, unless it abides in the vine, neither can you, unless you abide in Me. I am the vine, you are the branches. He who abides in Me, and I in him, bears much fruit; for without Me you can do nothing. If anyone does not abide in Me, he is cast out as a branch and is withered; and they gather them and throw them into the fire, and they are burned. If you abide in Me, and My words abide in you, you will ask what you desire, and it shall be done for you. By this*

My Father is glorified, that you bear much fruit; so you will be My disciples."

Many times I have waited and expected God to do something the way I understood or thought that He promised He would do it, only to have my dreams shattered repeatedly. Sometimes these things can be very confusing, and even devastating, but at the same time, God has a hold of our hearts. It is as though we cannot let go of the dream, or it will not let us go.

I contemplated this often. One time, of many times, when I was talking to God about these things, I asked for understanding. If it is not His idea or the dream or passion did not originate from His Spirit, why does He not just take it out of our hearts so we can forget about it? It hurts to long for something, to die to the desire or dream, and then to have God resurrect it again, only to shatter it again. Does He not know how hard it is to go through those disappointments repeatedly? Then I seemed to understand that it is God's way of bringing us to the end of ourselves. That is how we grow more and more in dependence upon Him, and we find out more and more that without Him we can do nothing.

We have to die to our old nature and desires so that we can reflect more and more of the new nature of Jesus. This shows in our attitude toward God and His Word. People see it in the way we treat them. If we love God, we will treat others well. The fear of the Lord is the beginning of knowledge and wisdom, and if we fear God, we will be careful how we treat people.

It seems to me that when God gives us a vision for our lives, the "carnality" has to be burned off of it first. Then when God brings it to pass it looks very different than the way we envisioned it before God put our character through the fire to bring us to maturity in Christ.

LaVergne, TN USA
10 November 2009
163668LV00004B/32/P